An Analysis of

Richard J. Herrnstein and Charles Murray's

The Bell Curve
Intelligence and Class Structure in American Life

Christine Ma

With

Michael Schapira

Published by Macat International Ltd
24:13 Coda Centre, 189 Munster Road, London SW6 6AW.

Distributed exclusively by Routledge
2 Park Square, Milton Park, Abingdon, Oxon OX14 4RN
711 Third Avenue, New York, NY 10017, USA

Routledge is an imprint of the Taylor & Francis Group, an informa business

www.macat.com
info@macat.com

Cataloguing in Publication Data
A catalogue record for this book is available from the British Library.
Library of Congress Cataloguing-in-Publication Data is available upon request.
Cover illustration: Etienne Gilfillan

ISBN 978-1-912303-59-5 (hardback)
ISBN 978-1-912128-48-8 (paperback)
ISBN 978-1-912282-47-0 (e-book)

Notice
The information in this book is designed to orientate readers of the work under analysis,
to elucidate and contextualise its key ideas and themes, and to aid in the development
of critical thinking skills. It is not meant to be used, nor should it be used, as a
substitute for original thinking or in place of original writing or research. References and
notes are provided for informational purposes and their presence does not constitute
endorsement of the information or opinions therein. This book is presented solely for
educational purposes. It is sold on the understanding that the publisher is not engaged
to provide any scholarly advice. The publisher has made every effort to ensure that
this book is accurate and up-to-date, but makes no warranties or representations with
regard to the completeness or reliability of the information it contains. The information
and the opinions provided herein are not guaranteed or warranted to produce particular
results and may not be suitable for students of every ability. The publisher shall not be
liable for any loss, damage or disruption arising from any errors or omissions, or from
the use of this book, including, but not limited to, special, incidental, consequential or
other damages caused, or alleged to have been caused, directly or indirectly, by the
information contained within.

CONTENTS

THE MACAT LIBRARY

The Macat Library is a series of unique academic explorations of seminal works in the humanities and social sciences – books and papers that have had a significant and widely recognised impact on their disciplines. It has been created to serve as much more than just a summary of what lies between the covers of a great book. It illuminates and explores the influences on, ideas of, and impact of that book. Our goal is to offer a learning resource that encourages critical thinking and fosters a better, deeper understanding of important ideas.

Each publication is divided into three Sections: Influences, Ideas, and Impact. Each Section has four Modules. These explore every important facet of the work, and the responses to it.

This Section-Module structure makes a Macat Library book easy to use, but it has another important feature. Because each Macat book is written to the same format, it is possible (and encouraged!) to cross-reference multiple Macat books along the same lines of inquiry or research. This allows the reader to open up interesting interdisciplinary pathways.

To further aid your reading, lists of glossary terms and people mentioned are included at the end of this book (these are indicated by an asterisk [*] throughout) – as well as a list of works cited.

Macat has worked with the University of Cambridge to identify the elements of critical thinking and understand the ways in which six different skills combine to enable effective thinking.
Three allow us to fully understand a problem; three more give us the tools to solve it. Together, these six skills make up the **PACIER** model of critical thinking. They are:

ANALYSIS – understanding how an argument is built
EVALUATION – exploring the strengths and weaknesses of an argument
INTERPRETATION – understanding issues of meaning

CREATIVE THINKING – coming up with new ideas and fresh connections
PROBLEM-SOLVING – producing strong solutions
REASONING – creating strong arguments

To find out more, visit **WWW.MACAT.COM.**

CRITICAL THINKING AND *THE BELL CURVE*

Primary critical thinking skill: REASONING
Secondary critical thinking skill: INTERPRETATION

Herrnstein & Murray's *The Bell Curve* is a deeply controversial text that raises serious issues about the stakes involved in reasoning and interpretation. The authors' central contention is that intelligence is the primary factor determining social outcomes for individuals – and that it is a better predictor of achievement than income, background or socioeconomic status. One of the major issues raised by the book was its discussion of 'racial differences in intelligence,' and its contention that there is a link between the low observed test scores and social outcomes for African-Americans and their lack of social attainment.

While the authors produce and interpret a great deal of data to back up their contentions, they ultimately fail to tackle the problem that neither 'intelligence' nor 'race' have widely accepted definitions in biology, anthropology or sociology. In consequence, the book it has been termed both 'racist' and 'pseudoscientific' thanks to what its critics see as both its faulty reasoning and its uncautious interpretation of evidence. The debate continues to this day, with academics on both sides engaged in fierce arguments over what can be argued from the data that Herrnstein and Murray used.

ABOUT THE AUTHORS OF THE ORIGINAL WORK

Richard J. Herrnstein was an American experimental psychologist. Born in 1930, he studied for his PhD at Harvard. He spent the rest of his working life at the university, becoming a lead researcher in the field of intelligence and human behavior. His collaboration with Charles Murray came at the end of his life. Shortly before *The Bell Curve* was published in 1994, Herrnstein died from lung cancer.

Charles Murray was born in 1943. He earned his PhD in political science at Massachusetts Institute of Technology, before going on to work at conservative think tanks. The author of several books, today Murray is one of America's most prominent conservative intellectuals. He has been at the American Enterprise Institute since 1990.

ABOUT THE AUTHORS OF THE ANALYSIS

Dr Christine Ma received her Ph.D. in Social Psychology from the University of California, Santa Barbara, in 2011. She was then a postdoctoral fellow at Harvard, working in the Psychology Department and the Harvard Kennedy School. She is currently an Assistant Professor of psychology at the University of Laverne, California.

Dr Michael Schapira earned his Ph.D. from the Teachers College at Columbia University for research into historical perspectives on the crisis of the university system. He is now on the faculty of the philosophy department at Hofstra University.

ABOUT MACAT

GREAT WORKS FOR CRITICAL THINKING

Macat is focused on making the ideas of the world's great thinkers accessible and comprehensible to everybody, everywhere, in ways that promote the development of enhanced critical thinking skills.

It works with leading academics from the world's top universities to produce new analyses that focus on the ideas and the impact of the most influential works ever written across a wide variety of academic disciplines. Each of the works that sit at the heart of its growing library is an enduring example of great thinking. But by setting them in context – and looking at the influences that shaped their authors, as well as the responses they provoked – Macat encourages readers to look at these classics and game-changers with fresh eyes. Readers learn to think, engage and challenge their ideas, rather than simply accepting them.

"Macat offers an amazing first-of-its-kind tool for interdisciplinary learning and research. Its focus on works that transformed their disciplines and its rigorous approach, drawing on the world's leading experts and educational institutions, opens up a world-class education to anyone."

Andreas Schleicher
Director for Education and Skills, Organisation for Economic Co-operation and Development

'Macat is taking on some of the major challenges in university education … They have drawn together a strong team of active academics who are producing teaching materials that are novel in the breadth of their approach.'

Prof Lord Broers,
former Vice-Chancellor of the University of Cambridge

'The Macat vision is exceptionally exciting. It focuses upon new modes of learning which analyse and explain seminal texts which have profoundly influenced world thinking and so social and economic development. It promotes the kind of critical thinking which is essential for any society and economy.
This is the learning of the future.'

Rt Hon Charles Clarke, former UK Secretary of State for Education

'The Macat analyses provide immediate access to the critical conversation surrounding the books that have shaped their respective discipline, which will make them an invaluable resource to all of those, students and teachers, working in the field.'

Professor William Tronzo, University of California at San Diego

WAYS IN TO THE TEXT

KEY POINTS

- Richard J. Herrnstein (1930–1994) was an American experimental psychologist;* Charles Murray (b. 1943) is an American conservative* political scientist* (a scholar of political behavior and systems of government, holding right-wing political beliefs).

- *The Bell Curve* argues that inequality in America is the result of varying levels of intelligence in the population. The authors say that intelligence is the best predictor of success in life.

- *The Bell Curve* is one of the most controversial books of the twentieth century. It claims that there are large differences in intelligence between ethnic groups* (subgroups who self-identify as Latino, black, white, or Asian, for example).

Who are Richard J. Herrnstein and Charles Murray?

The son of Hungarian Jewish immigrants, Richard J. Herrnstein, coauthor of *The Bell Curve: Intelligence and Class Structure in American Life* (1994), was born in 1930. He grew up in New York City, going on to Harvard University* to study for a PhD in experimental psychology.* At Harvard he worked with the famous psychologist B. F. Skinner.*[1] Skinner was a founder of the school of behaviorism, according to which all human behaviors are conditioned by rewards and punishments.[2] Later, however, after completing his PhD and joining the Harvard faculty as an experimental psychologist, Herrnstein moved away from Skinner's ideas. He became a leading researcher on intelligence and human behavior and claimed that innate (that is, inherent or inborn) biological forces contribute more to human behavior than one's environment.

Charles Murray was born in Newton, Iowa in 1943. He attended Harvard as an undergraduate and earned his PhD in political science at Massachusetts Institute of Technology.* During the 1980s he was a fellow at the Manhattan Institute for Policy Research,* a conservative think tank* (a privately funded organization conducting research and advocating for policy change). Here he wrote *Losing Ground: American Social Policy, 1950–1980* (1984), a book that made him famous in conservative intellectual circles. In 1990, Murray joined the American Enterprise Institute,* another conservative think tank in Washington, DC.

Four years later, Murray and Herrnstein collaborated on *The Bell Curve: Intelligence and Class Structure in American Life*. Shortly before the book was published, Herrnstein died of lung cancer. When *The Bell Curve* was met with both acclaim and controversy for its arguments and views, it was left to Murray to defend the book. He remains a staunch defender of the work's most controversial claims and has become one of America's most prominent conservative intellectuals.

What Does *The Bell Curve* Say?

The Bell Curve presents a controversial argument. The book's core idea is that social inequality in America can be explained by genes*— material inherited by children from their parents conferring biological characteristics. Herrnstein and Murray believe that intelligence is the most reliable predictor of success in life. At the top, the intellectual elite graduate from the best colleges and hold the best jobs. At the bottom, the intellectual underclass* suffers poverty, crime, and unemployment.

According to Herrnstein and Murray, intelligence is predominantly an inherited attribute. In the simplest terms, either you are born smart or you are not. Neither home environment nor schooling can change your genetic* inheritance.

The intellectual elite was fortunate enough to be born with good genes. The intellectual underclass was less fortunate in the genetic lottery. Between these two groups, *The Bell Curve* suggests, there is a growing gap, and there is little that the federal government can do about it. The authors believe that policies to improve opportunities for the lower classes will not achieve their goals because intelligence, not education or environment, determines people's success in life.

Herrnstein and Murray suggest that the intellectual divide in the population lies at the heart of the socioeconomic divide. An individual's socioeconomic status* is based on their economic status and their social position. This social gap (the divide between those who have wealth and influence and those who do not) also happens to mirror racial divides in America. Herrnstein and Murray link social position to genetic inheritance, which therefore links intelligence to race*—and offers an intellectual justification of the dominance of white people in American society.

When the book was first published these views about the social–racial divides in modern America were widely criticized. *The Bell Curve* became one of the most controversial publications of the 1990s. Three decades on, *The Bell Curve* is still controversial. Policy-makers and researchers continue to ask questions raised by the book:

- Is the intellectual underclass incapable of the same success as the   intellectual elite?*

- Is there a reason why African Americans are found in large numbers in impoverished communities?

- Is there nothing we can do to change this troubling reality?

By linking inequality, race, and intelligence, *The Bell Curve* provides a provocative explanation of how America's class structure formed in the twentieth century. It also provides a provocative explanation of why current social welfare* policies—policies designed to assist the poor by ensuring a measure of economic protection—are unlikely to change things.

The Bell Curve sold over 400,000 copies within months of its publication. Countless articles were published either denouncing or praising the book. A *New York Times* writer called the book "racial pornography."[3] Another writer praised Herrnstein and Murray for their courage in challenging political correctness.[4] *The Bell Curve* captured the attention of a divided nation. Few books since have placed such difficult and polarizing questions into the mainstream in such a way.

While much of the clamor has passed, questions about inequality, genes, and social policy remain. *The Bell Curve* gives readers an insight into how these questions will continue to challenge our notions of equality, race, and social justice.

Why Does *The Bell Curve* Matter?

It would be difficult to overstate the impact made by *The Bell Curve.* Perhaps the most debated book of 1994, it can be read as a portrait of America at its most divided. Critics of the book raced to disprove the link between intelligence, genetics, and race. Supporters were just as quick to claim that Herrnstein and Murray had put their finger on the true source of social disparities. A large portion of recent psychology* and social science* research looks at responses to the book. For this reason, one historian described *The Bell Curve* as a "phenomenon … more than a mere book."[5] Given the intensity of the response on all sides, it is important to see what Herrnstein and Murray actually say by looking at the original text.

The Bell Curve blends psychology (the study of the human mind and behavior), sociology* (the study of the history and nature of human society), and political science* (inquiry into political behavior and governance). For those interested in history and policymaking, the book is an important document in "the culture wars"* between American liberals and American conservatives in the 1980s and 1990s—a series of high-profile debates on issues including affirmative action* (policies designed to ease inequality by increasing the employment prospects of disadvantaged citizens), welfare reform, and educational standards. Those interested in psychology will find provocative theses on the nature of intelligence. Is it actually measurable? Does it explain human behavior? Can it change over time? The conservatism of Herrnstein and Murray will engage students of politics. *The Bell Curve* raises important questions about the politics of research. It presents a forceful argument against the federal government's ability to equalize life chances. Do changes in people's environments, through welfare or remedial education* programs (programs for underperforming, and often low-income, students), make them better students, parents, and workers?

Although scholars have failed to achieve consensus on *The Bell Curve's* scientific merits, and politicians continue to be divided on its policy recommendations, the book remains a testament to controversies surrounding intelligence, race, and class in twentieth-century America. In many ways, the debates over the nature of intelligence and its influence on behavior are still widespread. *The Bell Curve* suggests that social policies like affirmative action, universal preschool, and social welfare are ineffectual ways of solving the inequalities in American society. These policies continue to be objects of political debate. Given that, it is not surprising that the ideas in *The Bell Curve* continue to influence and inform opinions.

In 2012 Charles Murray published another book. *Coming Apart: The State of White America 1960–2010* [6] reintroduced many themes from *The Bell Curve*. The book triggered further debates about America's future. As inequalities persist, and in some cases deepen, the importance of these questions grows. Engaging with *The Bell Curve* gives readers a chance to work these issues out for themselves.

NOTES

1   B. F. Skinner, *Beyond Freedom and Dignity* (New York: Vintage Books, 1972).

2   James Watson, "Psychology as a Behaviorist Views It," *Psychological Review* 20 (1913): 158–77.

3   Bob Herbert, "In America; Throwing a Curve," *The New York Times*, October 26, 1994.

4   Daniel Seligman, "Trashing *The Bell Curve*," *The National Review*, 46, no. 23 (1994), 60–1.

5   Andrew Hartman, *A War for the Soul of America: A History of the Culture Wars* (Chicago: University of Chicago Press, 2015), 115.

6   Charles Murray, *Coming Apart: The State of White America 1960–2010* (New York: Random House, 2012).

SECTION 1
INFLUENCES

MODULE 1
THE AUTHOR AND THE HISTORICAL CONTEXT

KEY POINTS

- *The Bell Curve* remains one of the most hotly debated works of twentieth-century social science* (the academic study of human beings and social groups).

- Herrnstein and Murray's provocative thesis links intelligence with race* and social success. Their book continues to provide a controversial explanation for why racial divides persist in American society.

- Herrnstein and Murray published *The Bell Curve* at the height of America's "culture wars"* between political liberals* and political conservatives* during the 1980s and 1990s.

Why Read This Text?

Richard J. Herrnstein and Charles Murray's book *The Bell Curve: Intelligence and Class Structure in American Life* (1994) wades into some of the most troubled waters in contemporary America. The book argues that social inequality* between ethnic groups*—people of European, African, or indigenous American ancestry, for example— has a biological basis.

According to Herrnstein and Murray, widening inequality in America in income, educational attainment, and employment is largely explained by the differences in cognitive ability* (roughly, intelligence) between individuals. They argue that intelligence is decided by our genes.* As different ethnic groups have different genes, our intelligence is also affected by our ethnicity. This provocative argument raises debates about race, politics, economics, family, education, and equality.

> ❝ Our partnership has led to a more compelling intellectual adventure and a deeper friendship than we could have imagined. Authorship is alphabetical; the work was symbiotic. ❞
>
> Richard J. Herrnstein and Charles Murray, *The Bell Curve: Intelligence and Class Structure in American Life*

The Bell Curve was published in 1994, at the height of the American "culture wars*" of the 1980s and 1990s. These were high-profile debates between liberals and conservatives that spanned a whole range of contentious issues, including affirmative action* and welfare.* In this environment *The Bell Curve* was bound to elicit strong reactions.

An excerpt from the book was published on October 31, 1994 in *The New Republic*,* a magazine with liberal leanings. It was accompanied by comments. The respected American psychologist Richard Nisbett* praised Herrnstein and Murray for having "written a book that deals with extraordinarily important issues, many of which have been considered too explosive to discuss in the public arena yet need to be aired." Nonetheless, he disputed the idea that there was a scholarly consensus on their key claims.[1] Other commentators stated their "repulsion" by the idea that racial inequality has a biological basis.

The book sold over 400,000 copies. While its central thesis failed to gain mainstream support, explanations for the racial character of inequality in America continue to occupy scholars and politicians.

Authors' Lives

Richard J. Herrnstein was an experimental psychologist*—someone engaged in inquiry into the human mind and behavior—at Harvard University.* The son of Hungarian Jewish immigrants, he grew up in New York City, and studied psychology* at the City College of New York.* He obtained a PhD in experimental psychology* at Harvard,[2] where he studied with the famed psychologist B. F. Skinner.*[3] A behaviorist, Skinner argued that any and all human behavior is the direct result of conditioning—the rewards and consequences that result from the way we behave.[4] Over time, these external forces (the rewards and consequences) reinforce particular ways of behaving. Ironically, despite the fact that Herrnstein's academic training focused on the role of external forces in shaping behavior, in *The Bell Curve* he argues that innate biological forces (our genes) play a key role in the way we behave. Shortly before the publication of *The Bell Curve*, Herrnstein lost his life to lung cancer.

Charles Murray grew up in Newton, Iowa. As an undergraduate he studied history at Harvard, before obtaining his PhD in political science* at the Massachusetts Institute of Technology.* Murray went on to work for private research organizations, including the American Institutes for Research* and the right-wing think tank* the American Enterprise Institute.* His political stance is right wing and libertarian* (that is, he argues for individual freedom and is opposed to government intervention in society). Murray has clear ideas about the intractable nature of social hierarchies* (differences between individuals and groups in things such as income, educational achievement, and employment), and the futility of government programs designed to redress them. These ideas surface throughout *The Bell Curve*, especially in the concluding chapter of the book.

Authors' Backgrounds

Neither Herrnstein nor Murray came from an upper-class background. They acquired public influence and prestigious employment through America's elite institutions of higher education. Their success, one argument would have it, is down to the meritocratic* system, inside which advancement is based solely on achievement and ability—that is, merit. The notion of a meritocracy underpins the American belief that a combination of talent and resolve will be rewarded with recognition and success. Herrnstein developed this thesis in his early book *IQ in the Meritocracy* (1973), where he argued that the division of American society into a cognitive elite and a cognitive lower class reflects biological differences in intelligence.[5] As the American education system became more refined in the twentieth century, universities were able to select those with the most talent and place them in positions of power and prestige, regardless of their origins. This idea is restated in the first section of *The Bell Curve*, "The Emergence of a Cognitive Elite."*

The idea that merit alone leads to achievement came under heavy criticism from those active in civil rights and women's movements—political activity that began in the 1960s and 1970s and that is engaged with the struggle to achieve equal rights for minorities and women. In the 1980s and 1990s a new set of challenges arose. Many, among them those who argued for the benefits of multiculturalism,* asked how "merit" should be defined, and who should define it. A "multicultural" society is a society composed of different cultural traditions, commonly belonging to different ethnic groups; those valuing the possibilities of such a society argued that the type of success Herrnstein and Murray had attained was unattainable for those from minority groups,* as these groups lacked recognition and representation in universities.

These debates grew sharper as American living standards fell. The economic fortunes of the working class steadily declined in the 1970s and 1980s. In the 1980s and 1990s, African American communities were facing record levels of crime, homelessness, and youth unemployment, as well as a growing income gap with white Americans. In a meritocracy this though, highly unequal class structure could be conceived as a matter of individual responsibility. Was this position defensible?

NOTES

1   Richard Nisbett, "Blue Genes," *The New Republic,* October 31, 1994 (http://
    www.newrepublic.com/article/120890/tnr-staffers-and-others-respond-
    claims-bell-curve, accessed October 15, 2015).

2   Richard Baum, "Richard J. Herrnstein: A Memoir," *Behavioral Analysis* 17
    (1994): 201–6.

3   B. F. Skinner, *Beyond Freedom and Dignity* (New York: Vintage Books, 1972).

4   James Watson, "Psychology as a Behaviorist Views It," *Psychological Review*
    20 (1913): 158–77.

5   Richard J. Herrnstein, *IQ in the Meritocracy* (Boston: Little, Brown, 1973).

ACADEMIC CONTEXT

KEY POINTS

- *The Bell Curve* suggests that inherited intelligence has been overlooked as an explanation for the persistent inequalities in American society.

- By the 1990s inequality had become a growing concern for American social scientists.* They worried about the social disharmony that would follow from having a permanent underclass* — a section of society occupying the lowest position in the nation's social hierarchy for generations with little chances of advancement.

- This debate had ignored the issue of intelligence. There were fears that discussing the notion of intelligence would lead to explosive and incendiary theories about inherent differences between ethnic groups.*

The Work in its Context

Richard J. Herrnstein and Charles Murray's *The Bell Curve: Intelligence and Class Structure in American Life* addresses both academic and political concerns. This reflects the backgrounds of the two authors. Academically, *The Bell Curve* is an attempt to revive a tradition that dates back to the English naturalist Charles Darwin* and the theory of evolution* in its use of modern statistical analysis and testing mechanisms to determine the distribution of traits among a population. Herrnstein and Murray were testing the distribution of intelligence. Many researchers had avoided this topic because it carried overtones of scientific racism* (the use of scientific methods to argue that some racial groups are superior to others).

The idea that intelligence is a stable, inherited ability stems back to

> ❝ We are not indifferent to the ways in which this book, wrongly conceived, might do harm. We have worried about them from the day we set to work. But there can be no real progress in solving America's problems when they are as misperceived as they are today. ❞
>
> Richard J. Herrnstein and Charles Murray, *The Bell Curve: Intelligence and Class Structure in American Life*

the work of the nineteenth-century English statistician Sir Francis Galton.* In *Hereditary Genius*, published in 1869, Galton argued that intelligence ran in families.[1] Then, in the late nineteenth century, mental tests started being used to assess intelligence. In 1904 the English psychologist Charles Spearman* began using these tests to create a statistically quantifiable measure of general intellectual capacity, g.*[2] By the 1960s, there were some avid defendants of intelligence testing being used as a way of measuring underlying genetic*—inherent and inheritable—differences in mental ability. These included the American educational psychologist* Arthur Jensen,* who argued that it was futile to try to change an individual's intelligence. Jensen noted that because intelligence had a large genetic component, remedial education* programs targeting disadvantaged black schoolchildren would be ineffective at raising their IQ* (intelligence quotient) scores; the response to his article, published in the *Harvard Educational Review*, was both immediate and scathing.

The Bell Curve also addresses political issues. In 1964–5, the president of the United States, Lyndon Baines Johnson,* had introduced his "Great Society"* programs, a set of federally funded policies for reducing poverty and racial tension. They attempted to provide opportunities for those at the bottom of the class structure. But Herrnstein and Murray suggest that intelligence determines an individual's life chances. As cognitive ability cannot be changed, it places natural limitations on an individual's life chances. Their arguments challenge the wisdom of government spending in areas such as welfare.*

Overview of the Field

Modern studies of intelligence began with Charles Darwin, who stated that intelligence was a heritable*trait (a characteristic that can be passed on through the generations) and a major factor in human evolution.[3] This idea was developed by his cousin, Sir Francis Galton, who used the heritability of intelligence to explain the persistence of powerful families in Great Britain. But Galton and Darwin both lacked an accurate instrument to measure intelligence. As mental testing became more common in the nineteenth century, attempts were made to develop such an instrument. According to Herrnstein and Murray, the breakthrough was made in 1904 by the English statistician Charles Spearman, who was able to isolate what he called a "unitary mental factor" that varied consistently across mental tests. He called this factor g, for "general intelligence."

In the early twentieth century, tests measuring g were developed. These included the Stanford–Binet* test, which is still widely used today. However, in the 1960s scholars began to question whether intelligence was indeed heritable. There was a revival of scholarly interest in the psychologist B. F. Skinner's ideas about behaviorism, which suggest that humanity is malleable. The American educational psychologist Arthur Jensen rejected this, arguing that intelligence is heritable and can be correlated with educational performance. He said this is why many educational programs for struggling students— "remedial" programs—produce disappointing results.

Jensen's was a lone voice however. In the 1980s, skepticism toward g was intensified by the assertion that intelligence testing contained cultural biases against minorities. It was also undermined by the multiple intelligences* theory of the American developmental psychologist* Howard Gardner,* according to which there is not one single form of intelligence; instead, intelligence expresses itself in several different ways, such as musically, linguistically, or bodily. The American evolutionary biologist Stephen Jay Gould* united these two themes in his 1981 publication, *The Mismeasure of Man*.[4]

Academic Influences

Herrnstein worked alongside the great behavioral psychologist B. F. Skinner. Despite this, the strongest academic influences on *The Bell Curve* are the work of the English statistician Charles Spearman and the American educational psychologist Arthur Jensen. Much of the *Bell Curve* is dedicated to proving their key insights—namely that:

- g (a statistically quantifiable measure of general intellectual capacity) exists and can be measured

- g is heritable and correlates with behavior such as educational achievement.

Herrnstein and Murray are also indebted to the development of regression analysis*—a statistical method used to investigate the relationship between multiple variables. The English mathematician Karl Pearson*(1857–1936) was an early advocate of using regression analysis to measure the effects of intelligence on social behavior.

The Bell Curve is a politically conservative* book. In this it owes a debt to the Anglo-Irish statesman Edmund Burke* (1729–97). Burke was a critic of revolutionary political movements and the universal Enlightenment* principles that often serve as their rationale. The Enlightenment was an intellectual movement of seventeenth- and eighteenth-century Europe that emphasized rights, liberty, and reason. Burke opposed this movement, arguing that social stability comes through incremental improvements to societies, and that these incremental improvements respect the accumulated wisdom of national cultures and political institutions. While President Johnson's* "Great Society" programs were radical rather than revolutionary, Herrnstein and Murray express Burkean skepticism towards the policies that resulted from them. These policies included an expansion of welfare and heavy investment in remedial education. The authors *of The Bell Curve* are also critical of affirmative action* programs in higher education and hiring (policies designed to increase the representation of women and minorities in areas where they have been historically underrepresented).

Those with right-wing (conservative) political views reject affirmative action on the grounds that it is an infringement of equal opportunity; opposition to this policy has become a cause célèbre—a heated issue attracting a lot of public attention—among this group.

NOTES

1   Francis Galton, *Hereditary Genius* (London: Macmillan, 1982).

2   Charles Spearman, "General Intelligence, Objectively Determined and Measured," *American Journal of Psychology* 15 (1904): 201–29.

3   Charles Darwin, *The Origin of Species* (New York: P. F. Collier & Son, 1909).

4   Stephen Jay Gould, *The Mismeasure of Man* (New York: W. W. Norton, 1981).

THE PROBLEM

KEY POINTS

- *The Bell Curve* asks: Are persistent inequalities in American life due to the attributes of individual citizens or to structural causes such as unequal educational and economic opportunities?

- At the time it was published, many political scientists* and sociologists* argued that inequalities were socially derived; others argued that inequalities have a biological basis in terms of the heritability* of intelligence.

- Few scholars at the time looked to biology to explain social inequality* in such detail.

Core Question

Richard J. Herrnstein and Charles Murray's *The Bell Curve: Intelligence and Class Structure in American Life* addresses two linked questions: Is there a biological basis for the persistent inequalities in American life? And if there is, do differences in intelligence between ethnic groups* help explain the overrepresentation of minority groups* in poverty, crime, illegitimacy* (children born to unmarried parents), unemployment, and low educational achievement?

Herrnstein addressed the first question in a 1971 article he published in the American magazine *The Atlantic Monthly*, entitled "IQ."[1] In that article, and his subsequent book *IQ in the Meritocracy* (1973), Herrnstein argues that the stratification of American society is the direct result of inherited differences in cognitive ability* (something commonly understood as "intelligence"). He took a step toward answering the second question in his book *Crime and Human Nature* (1985), cowritten with Janes Q. Wilson, in which, again, he

> **❝** The egalitarian ideal of contemporary political theory underestimates the importance of the differences that separate human beings. It fails to come to grips with human variation. It overestimates the ability of political interventions to shape human character and capacities. **❞**
>
> Richard J. Herrnstein and Charles Murray, *The Bell Curve: Intelligence and Class Structure in American Life*

argued that criminal behavior can also be explained in large part by hereditary factors.[2] But it was not until the publication of *The Bell Curve* that the idea of inherited *racial* differences was developed.

Murray's earlier work had also touched on ideas that were developed more fully in *The Bell Curve.* In his book *Losing Ground: American Social Policy 1950–1980* (1984), Murray argued that federal programs aiming at helping disadvantaged groups actually hurt the groups they intended to help.[3] As for which policies best aided those at the bottom of the class structure, Murray argued that America's strong tradition of civil society*(nongovernmental voluntary organizations) was more cost effective and efficacious than federal interventions. *The Bell Curve* provides the scientific rationale for this belief. It claims that environmental changes—welfare* programs to reduce poverty, remedial education* to close achievement gaps, for example—can only marginally affect an individual's life chances.Their key potentials and limitations come through cognitive ability—a trait which, being heritable, can be passed from generation to generation.

The Participants

The English statistician Sir Francis Galton* was the first person to discuss the relationship between socioeconomic status* and intelligence. Subsequent participants in the debate developed the thesis that low intelligence, a heritable and measurable trait, was linked to deviancy. In the early and mid-twentieth century this idea helped to underpin the modern eugenics* movement—the attempt to use selective breeding or sterilization to promote or reduce particular traits within a population. In a famous legal case of 1927, *Buck v. Bell*, Justice Oliver Wendell Holmes*—a judge sitting on the highest legal institution of the United States, the Supreme Court* —upheld forced sterilization for citizens of low intelligence, famously stating that "three generations of imbeciles are enough."[4] But eugenics was also championed by the extremely right-wing Nazi* regime in Germany, irreparably damaging this line of research in the eyes of many researchers.

In policy circles, the Moynihan Report* of 1965, written by the American sociologist Daniel Patrick Moynihan,* looked at problems of poverty, illegitimacy, and crime in African American communities. Moynihan argued that high rates of children born out of marriage in impoverished black communities led to poor performance in education and employment, not the other way around.[5]

But in 1969 the American psychologist Arthur Jensen* argued against this. He said intelligence, not socioeconomic status,* best predicted future achievement. Jensen was challenged on two fronts. The Harvard psychologist Howard Gardner* argued that intelligence, being multi-faceted, is not an attribute that can be defined as a singular property. Poor performance in education only tells one side of the story. Intelligence in interpersonal relationships, creativity, and bodily activities are difficult to capture in test scores, but are equally important indicators of cognitive ability.[6] In his influential book *The Mismeasure of Man* (1981), the American evolutionary biologist Stephen Jay Gould* questioned Jensen's emphasis of nature over nurture.*[7] Gould argued that intelligence has a social basis and can improve or decline depending on environmental factors.

The Contemporary Debate

Growing inequality was an established theme when *The Bell Curve* was written. The American social scientist Christopher Jencks*[8] and the American sociologist William Julius Wilson*[9] had both written classic works on the subject, each mentioned in *The Bell Curve*. Jencks and Wilson sought explanations for inequality in structural forces, such as unequal access to quality education or employment. Herrnstein and Murray entered this debate, and challenged its parameters. Rather than focusing on structural causes of inequality, they explained inequality in terms of inherited biological differences. They courted a response from the public intellectual sphere by publishing an excerpt of *The Bell Curve* in the generally liberal American magazine *The New Republic.**

Such a gesture was common in the late 1980s and early 1990s, with the American world of letters embroiled in culture wars* between liberals and conservatives, fought over such issues as abortion, education, sexuality, and religion. Herrnstein and Murray were championed by political conservatives* for stating that behaviors had a biological basis. Until *The Bell Curve*, this idea was a political taboo*— that is, it was a topic generally avoided in political discourse. In America, the grand federal policies of the twentieth century, from the building programs of President Roosevelt's New Deal* to the Great Society* of President Johnson, largely reflected the liberal consensus that behavior was determined by environmental factors and inequality was a result of social and cultural forces. Herrnstein and Murray posed a strong challenge to this political and scholarly orthodoxy (generally accepted theory).

NOTES

1   Richard J. Herrnstein, "IQ," *The Atlantic Monthly* 228 (1971): 43–64.

2   James Q. Wilson and Richard J. *Herrnstein, Crime and Human Nature* (New York: Simon and Schuster, 1985).

3   Charles Murray, *Losing Ground: American Social Policy, 1950–1980* (New York: Basic Books, 1984).

4   *Buck v. Bell*, Superintendent of State Colony Epileptics and Feeble Minded, 274 U.S. 200 (1927).

5   http://www.dol.gov/oasam/programs/history/webid-meynihan.htm, accessed October 15, 2015.

6   Howard Gardner, *Frames of Mind: The Theory of Multiple Intelligences* (New York: Basic Books, 1983).

7   Steven Jay Gould, *The Mismeasure of Man* (New York: W. W. Norton, 1981).

8   Christopher Jencks *et al.*, *Inequality: A Reassessment of the Effect of Family and Schooling in America* (New York: Basic Books, 1972).

9   William Julius Wilson, *The Truly Disadvantaged: The Inner City, the Underclass, and Public Policy* (Chicago: University of Chicago Press, 1987).

THE AUTHORS' CONTRIBUTION

KEY POINTS

- The primary aim of *The Bell Curve* is to introduce intelligence as a variable into debates concerning inequality.

- This fed into debates about the effectiveness of programs in the United States aimed at reducing gaps in education, employment, and wealth.

- *The Bell Curve* brought new levels of intensity to debates about welfare,* affirmative action,* and remedial education* programs.

Authors' Aims

Richard J. Herrnstein and Charles Murray's *The Bell Curve: Intelligence and Class Structure in American Life* was influenced by the work of the American educational psychologist* Arthur Jensen.* Jensen had published several widely read papers on the correlation between cognitive ability* and various forms of achievement. In 1971, Herrnstein wrote an article linking Jensen's research on intelligence to issues of national policy. This laid the groundwork for his partnership with Charles Murray, a critic of the national welfare policy of the United States.[1]

Herrnstein and Murray aimed to challenge a growing orthodoxy that environment—the social, economic, and educational resources at people's disposal—was the primary factor in explaining social inequality* (the difference in wealth and living conditions, and so on, between the two ends of the social hierarchy*). According to Herrnstein, "there is evidence not only for the genetic* ingredients in mental capacity, but also in social status."[2] Herrnstein and Murray

66 Measures of intelligence have reliable statistical relationships with important social phenomena, but they are a limited tool for deciding what to make of any given individual. Repeat it we must, for one of the problems of writing about intelligence is how to remind readers often enough how little an IQ* score tells about whether the human being next to you is someone whom you will admire or cherish. This thing we know as IQ is important but not a synonym for human excellence. 99

Richard J. Herrnstein and Charles Murray, *The Bell Curve: Intelligence and Class Structure in American Life*

used the latest developments in statistical analysis to substantiate their claims. They also drew on a large bank of data that had been accumulated through the National Longitudinal Survey of Youth (NLSY).* This was a study started in 1979 by the American Bureau of Labor Statistics, collecting substantial information about a generation of youth employment.

The Bell Curve had an immediate impact, stimulating intense political and scholarly debates. The generally liberal* *New Republic** and the conservative* *National Review** magazines devoted entire issues to discussing the book's central themes. In addition, psychology* and social science* journals published many articles about Herrnstein and Murray's work. While the authors succeeded in introducing the variable of "intelligence" into national debate, their thesis linking race,* intelligence, and behavior has not gained mainstream acceptance. For many scholars the thesis is too simplistic to explain why inequality in America has such a striking racial component.

Approach

Herrnstein and Murray's major innovation was their use of data from the National Longitudinal Survey of Youth (NLSY). These data, gathered over a long period of time, captured measurements of intelligence known as "IQ" ("intelligence quotient") ratings, family background, and information about unemployment, low educational achievement, and crime within a statistically significant* set of 14–22-year-olds ("statistically significant" describes a set of data large enough to suggest a link between a variable and a measured phenomenon, such as behavior). The NLSY provided Murray and Herrnstein with the data set that could substantiate their claims. Using a statistical method known as regression analysis,* useful for considering the relationship between many variables, they could evaluate (and eventually reject) the thesis that environmental factors explained social behavior better than the biological factor of cognitive ability.

Herrnstein and Murray wanted the ideas offered in *The Bell Curve* to shape ongoing discussions about inequality in America and to influence policymaking. They ask one key question: Why has the gap between the most and least advantaged not closed, despite large investments in social programs? The book begins by describing the rise of a "cognitive elite"*—those who have gained positions of prestige and power through meritocratic* means. Talent and hard work, then, allow this cognitive elite to access opportunities in education and employment that allow them to prosper. This process, the authors argue, has "stratified America according to cognitive ability," leaving those with lower intelligence on the bottom of the social ladder. Herrnstein and Murray's message is that a society stratified on the basis of cognitive ability differs from a society only divided by socioeconomic* factors. As a result, it requires different social policies.

The book's structure shows that the authors wanted this political message to take center stage. They establish the political implications of their arguments long before introducing their most controversial claim—that the biological inheritance of different ethnic groups means they have differing levels of cognitive ability. This provocative idea is only found in the third section of the book.

Contribution in Context

Race was inserted into debates about intelligence and social policy in the nineteenth century. In the first half of the twentieth century the eugenics* movement, founded on the idea that selective breeding through means such as sterilization might "improve" a nation or the human species, fused conservative social policies with a biological view of differences in individual cognitive abilities. Interest in a biological basis for intelligence was reintroduced in the post–World War II* period by the work of the American educational psychologist Arthur Jensen. In 1969 he published an article in the *Harvard Educational Review* called "How Much Can We Boost IQ and Scholastic Achievement?"[3] But *The Bell Curve* provided the most forceful articulation of these ideas in the period following World War II. Herrnstein and Murray's work was a challenge to welfare policy, affirmative action programs in higher education and hiring procedures, and remedial education. These areas produced some of the most hotly contested debates in contemporary society.

The Bell Curve has become an important touchstone for modern conservatism. It defends meritocracy and challenges the wisdom of federal policy interventions. In this regard it is a natural synthesis of both Herrnstein and Murray's prior work, particularly Herrnstein's *IQ in the Meritocracy* (1973) and Murray's *Losing Ground* (1984). Due to the tensions produced by the culture wars* in America in the 1980s and 1990s, the tone of *The Bell Curve* is heightened. It contains many warnings such as the following: "Mounting evidence indicates that demographic trends are exerting downward pressure on the distribution of cognitive ability in the United States and that the pressures are strong enough to have social consequences."[4]

According to Herrnstein and Murray, policies that focus solely on environmental factors must be changed or they will continue to fall short of their goals.

NOTES

1   Charles Murray, *Losing Ground: American Social Policy, 1950–1980* (New York: Basic Books, 1984).

2   Richard J. Herrnstein, "On Challenging an Orthodoxy," *Commentary*, April 1, 1973 (https://www.commentarymagazine.com/articles/on-challenging-an-orthodoxy/, accessed October 15, 2015).

3   Arthur Jensen, "How Much Can We Boost IQ and Scholastic Achievement?" *Harvard Educational Review* 39 (1969): 1–123.

4   Richard J. Herrnstein and Charles Murray, *The Bell Curve: Intelligence and Class Structure in American Life* (New York: Basic Books, 1994), 341.

SECTION 2
IDEAS

MAIN IDEAS

KEY POINTS

- Herrnstein and Murray attempt to explain a link between intelligence and social inequality* in American society. They explore the relationships between the intelligence rating known as IQ* and achievement, IQ and race,* and genetics* and environment.

- *The Bell Curve* argues that intelligence, not socioeconomic status,* is the most important predictor of life success.

- Herrnstein and Murray make policy recommendations on the basis that inborn differences in cognitive ability* (for them, meaning "intelligence") limit the potential gains made for individuals by interventions in their environment.

Key Themes

Richard J. Herrnstein and Charles Murray begin *The Bell Curve: Intelligence and Class Structure in American Life* with the assertion that "the word *intelligence* describes something real and … varies from person to person." They also claim that intelligence varies from one ethnic group* to another.* (They prefer the term "ethnicity" to "race" because of the difficulties in defining race. The ethnic groups they study are Latinos, blacks, whites (i.e. non-Latino whites), and Asians, and all categories are based on the self-identification of participants in the National Longitudinal Study of Labor Market Experience of Youth [NLSY].*)

Herrnstein and Murray acknowledge that their claim about intelligence is a controversial one, but they say, nevertheless, that intelligence must be taken into account when formulating public policy. To do otherwise is "to fight a demographic headwind" in which

> **❝** To try to come to grips with the nation's problems without understanding the role of intelligence is to see through the glass darkly indeed, to grope with symptoms instead of causes, to stumble into supposed remedies that have no chance of working. **❞**
>
> Richard J. Herrnstein and Charles Murray, *The Bell Curve: Intelligence and Class Structure in American Life*

the biological factor of intelligence will frustrate attempts to equalize society through federal policies.[1] Underlying their argument is the assumption that intelligence is largely a matter of genetic* inheritance. As such, it cannot be substantially changed by interventions in people's home and learning environments. For Herrnstein and Murray, this insight helps explain the class structure of American society.

Herrnstein and Murray believe that it is politics, not science, that prevents policy-makers from considering the role of intelligence in social inequality. Put more bluntly, they believe that researchers and policy-makers have steered clear of these themes for fear of being labeled racist. Nevertheless, they argue that researchers of intelligence have reached consensus on the following six broad conclusions:

- There is a "general factor of cognitive ability," or "*g*,"* which differs among human beings.

- Modern intelligence tests (IQ tests) are designed to accurately measure cognitive ability.

- High IQ is generally indicative of the everyday meaning of "smart" or "intelligent."

- IQ scores are fairly constant over a person's life.

- Modern IQ tests are unbiased against minority groups.*

- Cognitive ability is a heritable* trait, within certain boundaries when coupled with environmental factors.

The Bell Curve is divided into four sections that build upon these conclusions:

- Section I establishes the link between cognitive ability and social goods such as educational attainment, high income, and occupational prestige.

- Section II attributes social ills such as poverty, crime, unemployment, and poor educational attainment to low cognitive ability. It limits the analysis to white Americans to insulate the authors from charges of racist motivations in later analysis concerning race.

- Section III broadens the analysis to the "national context." This section claims that differences in the average intelligence of ethnic groups shows a correlation between race, intelligence, and social achievement.

- Section IV, "Living Together," puts forth a set of policy recommendations. These claim to further the ends of a just, equitable, and democratic society.

Exploring the Ideas

In *The Bell Curve* Herrnstein and Murray propose a radical redefinition of the term "class."* The concept of class is central to debates about welfare,* education, and educational and employment outcomes. When Herrnstein and Murray were writing, politicians and social scientists* used socioeconomic status* (SES) to determine where interventions should be made. The government targeted those at the lower end of the SES spectrum with a range of economic and political programs. But rather than focusing on SES, Herrnstein and Murray argue that we should consider "cognitive classes" because cognitive ability explains social differences.

Herrnstein and Murray discuss the social programs that grew in the US out of President Lyndon Baines Johnson's* "War on Poverty"* of 1964, noting that these programs neither closed the income gaps between rich and poor nor stemmed the concentration of poverty and crime in impoverished, primarily African American urban communities. They argue that differences in cognitive ability mean the chances of success for these social programs are radically reduced. As a result, expensive federal programs can only make marginal changes in life outcomes.

The concluding section of *The Bell Curve* moves toward a more affirmative picture of America's future. It begins with a call for realistic expectations about how much government policies can aim to reduce social inequalities. Herrnstein and Murray plead for a return to investment in the "American Dream"*—the idea that hard work coupled with strong resolve will allow individuals to achieve success. They argue that meaningful social change is slow, but that governments can set the country on the right course. As an example of that, Herrnstein and Murray highlight the Civil Rights Act of 1964,* which prevented discrimination on the basis of race, color, religion, sex, or national origin. Legislation that fights discrimination helps to create opportunities for all Americans to contribute meaningfully to their communities.

Language and Expression

The Bell Curve is an accessible work, as long as one has the patience to wade through its graphs and charts. Herrnstein and Murray establish their correlation between cognitive ability and social inequality largely through an analysis of the NLSY. This study began in 1979 and tracked the socioeconomic status, educational and occupational achievement, work history, family formation, and cognitive ability of a statistically significant* set of 14–22-year-olds. The pattern of Herrnstein and Murray's analysis becomes clear early in the book and their findings remain consistent throughout.

The book is intended for a broad, nonspecialist audience. The authors even provide a primer on statistical analysis in Appendix 1. They are clear in their desire to redefine the American class structure in terms of intelligence rather than socioeconomic status. To do this, they coin terms such as "the cognitive elite"* and "cognitive classes."* The final section of the book explores the political implications of the analysis, but Herrnstein and Murray—writing for the public as well as for politicians and academics—are careful not to get mired in detailed policy recommendations. They settle on a simple, comprehensible formula: "The vast majority of Americans can run their lives just fine and policy should above all be constructed so that it permits them to do so."[2]

NOTES

1   Richard J. Herrnstein and Charles A. Murray, *The Bell Curve: Intelligence and Class Structure in American Life* (New York: Basic Books, 1994), 342.

2   Herrnstein and Murray, *The Bell Curve*, 550.

MODULE 6
SECONDARY IDEAS

KEY POINTS

- *The Bell Curve* offers an account of social stratification in twentieth-century America along cognitive rather than economic class* lines.

- Continuing debates over higher education and educational reform reflect Herrnstein and Murray's claim that education stratifies society into cognitive classes.*

- Herrnstein and Murray speculate about the long-term effects of declining mean IQ* scores in the twenty-first century, which was largely ignored by other late-twentieth-century scholars. A mean average is calculated by adding a set of numbers (here, IQ scores) and dividing by the total number in that set (here, the number of people tested for IQ).

Other Ideas

Richard J. Herrnstein and Charles Murray's *The Bell Curve: Intelligence and Class Structure in American Life* is most often associated with its controversial claims about racial differences in cognitive ability. However, the book also contains several interesting themes about the development of the United States in the twentieth century.

The first section of the book describes "the emergence of a cognitive elite"* over the twentieth century. This is explained partially by the consolidation of elite* colleges and universities at the top of the educational ladder, and partially by the needs of a complex technological society. The effect of this has been to lead to further "cognitive partitioning"*—isolating the cognitive classes from one another in educational and employment settings (for example, in the growing separation between skilled and unskilled labor in large firms).

> ❝ As America opened access to higher education, it opened up as well a revolution in the way that the American population sorted itself and divided itself. Three successively more efficient sorting processes were at work: the college population grew, it was recruited by cognitive ability* more efficiently, and then it was further sorted among the colleges. ❞
>
> Richard J. Herrnstein and Charles Murray, *The Bell Curve: Intelligence and Class Structure in American Life*

Consequently, members of different cognitive classes rarely interact in any practical way.

This introduces a broader theme of social disharmony. Murray returns to this in his 2012 book *Coming Apart: The State of White America 1960–2010*.[1] In *The Bell Curve*, Herrnstein and Murray praise the mechanisms, such as college admission, that create a meritocratic* society, because the needs of a complex, technological society have to be met by placing the brightest people in the most complex positions. However, one of its effects is to concentrate those with less cognitive ability in impoverished communities.

Here *The Bell Curve* explores Social Darwinism*—the application to human society of the ideas first proposed by the nineteenth-century naturalist Charles Darwin concerning the evolutionary principle of the "survival of the fittest." Herrnstein and Murray speculate about the long-term effects of "dysgenic pressure"* (the gradual reduction of IQ in a population due to changes in the gene pool). They argue that this happens because those with low cognitive ability have higher birth rates than the cognitive elite.[2]

Exploring the Ideas

For Herrnstein and Murray, the rise of the cognitive elite is a twentieth-century success story. They believe that it will prove essential for responding to the seismic shifts in the economy caused by advances in technology:"Technology has increased the economic value of intelligence. As robots replace factory workers, the factory workers' jobs vanish, but new jobs pop up for people who can design and repair robots."[3]

The concentration of workers with high scores in intelligence tests in certain occupations, whether they be associated with technology, law, education, or finance, is presented as a precondition for long-term economic viability. "The more complex a society becomes," state Herrnstein and Murray, "the more valuable are the people who are especially good at dealing with complexity."[4]

The policy implications of this are elaborated in the final section of the book. This argues against affirmative action* policies in higher education and hiring policies. Herrnstein and Murray believe that a meritocratic system, which rewards talent and hard work, is best placed to meet the needs of a technological society. They argue that their work provides a scientific basis to justify this belief.

Herrnstein and Murray also discuss the need for policies to deal with the reality of dysgenic pressure. "Improved health, education, and childhood interventions may hide the demographic effects [of dysgenic pressure]," they argue, but policies associated with these improvements "would be much more effective if they did not have to fight a demographic headwind."[5] In other words, low cognitive ability will continue to define the lower ends of the class structure. This has to be recognized if effective policies are to be created for dealing with it. These policies will be different to those that attempt to promote educational and economic achievement through interventions in people's environment.

Overlooked

Herrnstein and Murray's thesis relating intelligence first to social success and then to race* was so provocative it led many readers to overlook their account of how the United States had divided into cognitive classes. Yet in many respects their ideas reflect the educational priorities of the United States of the early twenty-first century. Curricula at all levels emphasize skills related to STEM disciplines (science, technology, engineering, and math). The influx of funding for STEM disciplines and the attempt to distribute these skills widely across the American population has become conventional wisdom in policy circles. The belief is that STEM skills are needed to ensure America remains competitive within the global economy. Herrnstein and Murray suggest that jobs are becoming increasingly complex and that workers with high cognitive ability need to be identified and cultivated to do these jobs. They also suggest that there needs to be renewed investment in gifted and talented programs* (special accelerated educational programs for students who demonstrate very high achievement levels at an early age). In their view, these programs suffered a reduction in funding when the emphasis was placed on remedial education* programs (programs for people who underperform educationally). This idea has recently been championed by the US educator Frederick Hess,* Murray's colleague at the American Enterprise Institute,* a right-wing policy body.[6]

Herrnstein and Murray's ideas about the decline of average (mean) IQ scores have been heavily criticized as a modern version of Social Darwinism. But it could be noted that the United States has implemented policies, such as the H1–B visa* program, that are designed to attract intellectual talent from other nations to take up positions requiring highly skilled workers; it has been argued that these bear some resemblance to the idea of altering the distribution of intelligence within the population.[7] Herrnstein and Murray write that their "central thought about immigration is that present policy assumes an indifference to the individual characteristics of immigrants that no society can indefinitely maintain without danger."[8] This call to introduce certain forms of discrimination into immigration policy reflects the attempt to draw high-IQ immigrants into America through visa programs.

NOTES

1 Charles Murray, *Coming Apart: The State of White America 1960–2010* (New York: Random House, 2012).

2 Richard J. Herrnstein and Charles A. Murray, *The Bell Curve: Intelligence and Class Structure in American Life* (New York: Basic Books, 1994), 535–41.

3 Herrnstein and Murray, *The Bell Curve*, 98.

4 Herrnstein and Murray, *The Bell Curve*, 99.

5 Herrnstein and Murray, *The Bell Curve*, 341–2.

6 Frederick Hess, "America's Future Depends on Gifted and Talented Students," *New York Times*, June 4, 2014 (http://www.nytimes.com/roomfordebate/2014/06/03/are-new-york-citys-gifted-classrooms-useful-or-harmful/americas-future-depends-on-gifted-students, accessed October 15, 2015).

7 Julia Preston, "Pink Slips at Disney. But First, Training Foreign Replacements," *New York* Times, June 3, 2015 (http://www.nytimes.com/2015/06/04/us/last-task-after-layoff-at-disney-train-foreign-replacements.html, accessed October 15, 2015).

8 Herrnstein and Murray, *The Bell Curve*, 549.

ACHIEVEMENT

KEY POINTS

- *The Bell Curve* did not succeed in achieving a scholarly consensus that intelligence was the best predictor of success.

- Herrnstein and Murray published their book at the height of the "culture wars"* of the 1980s and 1990s. While this was a time when controversial theses attracted great public attention, these "wars" also served to limit the book's success.

- Critics attacked the methodology of *The Bell Curve* and the way the statistical analysis was used as a basis for policy recommendations.

Assessing the Argument

Richard J. Herrnstein and Charles Murray's *The Bell Curve: Intelligence and Class Structure in American Life* argues that there is a biological basis for differences in achievement among different social groups in America. At the book's heart is the question: "How and why did these differences come to exist in modern America?" Herrnstein and Murray focus on the core causes of the nation's biggest problems—poverty, underachievement, unemployment, divorce, illegitimacy,* and crime.

This issue of difference in intellectual ability between groups is important for two reasons:

- Understanding the causes of social division can reveal the underlying forces behind humanity's greatest challenges, such as poverty, underachievement, and crime.

> ❝ Our intellectual landscape has been disrupted by the equivalent of an earthquake and, as the ground settles, intellectuals are looking around nervously and bracing themselves. At such times, the best policy is to heed the evidence that leads toward truth. ❞
>
> Michael Novak, "Sins of the Cognitive Elite," *National Review*

- Solving the question of why different groups experience different outcomes can present new policy solutions.

Herrnstein and Murray are interested in the causes rather than the symptoms of America's social problems. They argue that intelligence has been ignored for too long and that without considering it, it is impossible to understand the nation's current social challenges. They want to understand the roots of inequality in order to find new ways of solving the social challenges it creates. Much of their book is dedicated to describing the symptoms of America's class* divide—the changing face of higher education and occupations, the social ills that characterize the lower social classes, the racial differences shown in intelligence testing and academic performance. The impetus for this narrative, however, is to show that intelligence is the underlying force that explains and accounts for this.

Herrnstein and Murray remain thematically consistent and offer a broad set of statistical analyses to support their work. But their methodology and their policy recommendations received intense criticism from those on the political left wing. The intensity and volume of this criticism can be attributed to the culture wars between liberals* and conservatives,* which were at their height when *The Bell Curve* was published. The criticism prevented Herrnstein and Murray from achieving broad consensus about their claims.

Achievement in Context

Herrnstein and Murray tried to forestall accusations of racism. *The Bell Curve* contains several statements such as: "Measures of intelligence have reliable statistical relationships with important social phenomena, but they are a limited tool for deciding what to make of any given individual ... IQ* is important but not a synonym [that is, another term] for human excellence."[1]

The Bell Curve could not avoid charges of inciting racial tension. The American evolutionary biologist Stephen Jay Gould* charged Herrnstein and Murray with "disingenuousness of content" in denying that differences in cognitive ability* between ethnic groups* say anything statistically significant* about individuals in those racial groups.[2] There are more than 800 pages in *The Bell Curve*, and Gould notes that equal space is given to intelligence and race.* This alone suggests that race is a major theme in the book.

Two years after *The Bell Curve* was published, the Republicans (the largest right-wing party in the United States) were in ascendency in Congress, one of the US's principal lawmaking bodies. Along with the centrist Democrat President Bill Clinton,* they passed a sweeping Welfare Reform* program that reduced the role of the federal government in providing economic aid to poor communities—a policy decision that in some ways mirrored Herrnstein and Murray's recommendations. Ronald Reagan,* a Republican who served as president between 1981 and 1989, had made the curtailment of federal poverty reduction and education programs a cornerstone of his economic policy. However, it is significant that this policy shift from the expansive "Great Society" programs* of the 1960s to a reduced federal role also occurred within the Democratic party. Bill Clinton even cited Charles Murray as an influence in his thinking about welfare reform.[3]

Limitations

Herrnstein and Murray present widening inequality along racial and class lines as a feature of US development in the twentieth century. This widening inequality has occurred despite decades of federal programs aimed at improving the lives of impoverished groups; this is a challenging reality for many scholars and policy-makers. *The Bell Curve* introduces a new set of ideas about inequality, all of which are testable hypotheses.

While Herrnstein and Murray called for further research into their ideas that attempted to address far-reaching problems, their answers proved too reductive (or simplistic) for many readers.[4] Stephen Jay Gould lamented that *The Bell Curve*'s "success in winning attention must reflect the depressing temper of our time—a historical moment of unprecedented ungenerosity, when a mood for slashing social programs can be abetted by an argument that beneficiaries cannot be helped, owing to the inborn cognitive limits expressed as low IQ scores."[5]

On the other side of the political divide from Gould, the US philosopher Michael Novak* wrote in the conservative magazine the *National Review*: "The problem with [federal] policy today is that on at least three matters—IQ, heritability,* and human nature—the rules we have lived under for some decades now are evasion, euphemism [substitution of a more acceptable term], and taboo [a forbidden subject]."[6]

The Bell Curve failed to bridge the sharp partisan divides (disagreements biased along party lines) between liberals and conservatives. In this respect, it stands as an emblematic document of the culture wars. This political impasse has resulted in a weakening of support for biological and cultural explanations for inequality. Most scholars now prefer structural and economic approaches.[7]

NOTES

1   Richard J. Herrnstein and Charles A. Murray, *The Bell Curve: Intelligence and Class Structure in American Life* (New York: Basic Books, 1994), 21.

2   Stephen Jay Gould, *The Mismeasure of Man* (revised and expanded edition) (New York: W. W. Norton, 1996), 370.

3   http://www.clintonlibrary.gov/assets/storage/Research-Digital-Library/dpc/reed-welfare/20/612964–meetings-2.pdf, accessed October 30, 2015.

4   Brigitte Berger, "Methodological Fetishism," *National Review*, 46, no. 23 (1994), 54.

5   Gould, *The Mismeasure of Man*, 367.

6   Michael Novak, "Sins of the Cognitive Elite," *The National Review*, 46, no. 23 (1994), 58.

7   See e.g. Thomas Piketty, *Capital in the 21st Century* (Boston: Belknap Press, 2014).

MODULE 8
PLACE IN THE AUTHORS' WORK

KEY POINTS

- *The Bell Curve* marks the culmination of Herrnstein's decades of research on the heritability* of intelligence.

- Herrnstein's death just before the publication of *The Bell Curve* means the book is the only major collaboration between the two authors.

- The enduring role of *The Bell Curve* in political debates, and the intensity with which its ideas were received, make it the authors' best-known work.

Positioning

Richard J. Herrnstein and Charles Murray had both written earlier works that hinted at the themes they made explicit in *The Bell Curve: Intelligence and Class Structure in American Life*. Herrnstein had been discussing the meritocracy* since the early 1970s, first in an article for the *Atlantic Monthly* and then in his book, *IQ and the Meritocracy*. He believed that the meritocracy reflects cognitive differences within the population. It operates by routing talented students through elite* institutions of higher education, which then place them in jobs of power and significant complexity.[1]

Murray articulated a consistent political agenda throughout his career. In books such as *Apollo: the Race to the Moon,*[2] (1989), *What it Means to be a Libertarian* (1996),[3] and *By the People: Rebuilding Liberty without Permission,*[4] (2015) he opposes welfare* and affirmative action.* He remains an active libertarian* intellectual. His 2012 book *Coming Apart: The State of White American 1960–2010*[5] continues many of the policy suggestions made at the end of *The Bell Curve*, albeit without *The Bell Curve*'s explicit focus on race.*

> **❝ Despite the forbidding air that envelops the topic, ethnic differences in cognitive ability* are neither surprising nor in doubt. Large human populations differ in many ways, both cultural and biological. ❞**
>
> Richard J. Herrnstein and Charles Murray, *The Bell Curve: Intelligence and Class Structure in American Life*

In a 2014 interview Murray looked back at the legacy of *The Bell Curve* and lamented that "the social sciences* have been in the grip of a political orthodoxy [generally accepted theory] that has had only the most tenuous connection with empirical reality [verifiable facts], and too many social scientists think that threats to the orthodoxy should be suppressed by any means necessary."[6] His suggestion is that *The Bell Curve*'s ideas have been ignored because social scientists fear being labeled racist. Herrnstein and Murray positioned their work in opposition to what they saw as political liberal orthodoxies—but failed to sway their critics.

Integration

Herrnstein and Murray published *The Bell Curve* in 1994. Questions about the nature of human intelligence had been around since the time of the English naturalist Charles Darwin,*and various other scholars had put forth arguments about the biological basis of intelligence.[7] Many ways of measuring intelligence had been developed since the late 1800s, but by the 1990s the issue of racial differences was increasingly becoming a question of interest.[8] At the same time, there were ongoing political disputes over support and funding for government programs to tackle social problems. There was opposition to affirmative action programs, which were designed to increase the representation of disadvantaged students. There was also opposition to social welfare programs designed to alleviate poverty. The racially charged debate over intelligence and the political debate over government-funded social programs culminated with the publication of *The Bell Curve*, which catapulted these controversies into the public eye.

Some academics are restricted in what they can say, either because their books have to pass through a stringent peer-review process (according to which, others working in the researcher's academic field read a work to endorse or reject its findings) before it is published or because they are not yet well established in their careers. Herrnstein and Murray did not face either of these restrictions. *The Bell Curve* was directed at the public at large rather than at a strictly academic audience, which meant that it was not subject to the peer-review process that typically accompanies published journal articles. In addition, both authors were well established within their fields and their careers—Herrnstein as a tenured professor, and Murray as a well-respected figure and long-standing contributor to a conservative* think tank.* This allowed them to express themselves freely and to synthesize decades of research for a large audience.

Significance
Although it was the only substantial collaboration between Herrnstein and Murray, *The Bell Curve* is the most important work of both authors. On its publication in 1994, it established them as household names. For researchers in the fields of psychology* and genetics* the book has become a controversial aspect of Herrnstein's legacy[9] on account of the way in which it applies scholarly discussions on the heritability of intelligence to social and political issues.

Looking beyond the particular theses advanced in *The Bell Curve*, the book's enduring significance resides in the relationship it builds between its use of empirical inquiry (that is, data verifiable by observation) and political considerations. Many readers found it deeply pessimistic in its suggestion of a form of genetic determinism*—

the principle that genes determine behavior and social outcomes come what may—that the authors claim is largely beyond the power of social policies to influence.

Charles Murray argues that because this conclusion may be drawn from *The Bell Curve*, social scientists have dismissed the book. He accuses them of "cowardice" and "corruption" for doing so.[10] Referencing theology, the study of religious ideas, and eschatology, the aspect of theology concerned with death and the destiny of the soul, the conservative philosopher Michael Novak* mocks denunciations of the book by those on the political left. He writes that for them, "*The Bell Curve*'s message cannot be true, because much more is at stake than a particular set of arguments from psychological science. A this-worldly eschatological hope is at stake. The sin attributed to Herrnstein and Murray is theological: they destroy hope."[11]

This response to the negative reception that *The Bell Curve* received from the left wing shows how responses to the book were split down political lines. Controversies over research that draws unorthodox conclusions continue. So does the idea that Murray paints a gloomy picture of America's future.[12]

NOTES

1 Richard J. Herrnstein, "IQ," *The Atlantic Monthly* 228 (1971): 43–64.

2 Charles Murray and Catherine Bly Cox, *Apollo: The Race to the Moon* (New York: Touchstone Books, 1989).

3 Charles Murray, *What it Means to be a Libertarian*. New York: Broadway Books, 1997.

4 Charles Murray, *By the People: Rebuilding Liberty Without Permission*. New York: Crown Forum, 2015.

5 See Charles Murray, *Coming Apart: The State of White America 1960–2010* (New York: Random House, 2012).

6   "The Bell Curve 20 Years Later: A Q & A with Charles Murray" (https://www.aei.org/publication/bell-curve-20–years-later-qa-charles-murray/, accessed October 15, 2015).

7   Arthur Jensen, "How Much Can We Boost IQ and Scholastic Achievement?" *Harvard Educational Review* 39 (1969): 1–123.

8   Richard Fletcher and John Hattie, *Intelligence and Intelligence Testing* (New York: Routledge, 2011), 13–30.

9   Daniel Goleman, "Richard Herrnstein, 64, Dies; Backed Nature Over Nurture," *The New York Times*, September 16, 1994.

10 "The Bell Curve 20 Years Later."

11 Michael Novak, "Sins of the Cognitive Elite," *The National Review*, 46, no 23 (1994), 58.

12 Andrew Hacker, "The White Plight," *New York Review of Books*, May 10, 2012 (http://www.nybooks.com/articles/archives/2012/may/10/white-plight/, accessed October 15, 2015).

11 Tainter, "Global Change," 131.

SECTION 3
IMPACT

MODULE 9
THE FIRST RESPONSES

KEY POINTS

- Critics of *The Bell Curve* view the book as racist and a work of pseudo-science* (that is, that despite its claims to be based on the scientific method, it fails the test of scientific scrutiny). Those who were more sympathetic to the project praised Herrnstein and Murray for challenging political and scholarly orthodoxies.

- Charles Murray remains a strong defender of *The Bell Curve*. He argues that the book's critics either misread its arguments or attack it for political reasons.

- As evidenced by *The Bell Curve's* intense, public, and highly polarized reception, the book became part of the "culture wars"* between American liberals* and conservatives.*

Criticism

Richard J. Herrnstein and Charles Murray's *The Bell Curve: Intelligence and Class Structure in American Life* generated an intense response from both sides of the political spectrum. Within one year from the initial publication of *The Bell Curve*, two volumes of responses had been published.[1]

"Charles Murray has achieved the impossible, or at least the highly improbable," wrote the libertarian* commentator Frank Miele* in the magazine the *Skeptic*. "He has coauthored an 845-page book, filled with figures, tables, references, and appendices loaded with multiple regression analyses, that is also the most controversial book in America."[2] *The New York Times* columnist Bob Herbert* called the work "a scabrous [that is, scandalous] piece of racial pornography masquerading as serious scholarship."[3] Conversely, the writer and editor Daniel Seligman* defended Herrnstein and Murray in the

> ❝ Soon after publication, more than mere book, *The Bell Curve* became a phenomenon dissected in most major national publications. Pundits of every ideological stripe weighed in on the debate. ❞
>
> Andrew Hartman, *A War for the Soul of America: A History of the Culture Wars*

National Review; for him, liberal "arguments [over human malleability] were crumbling even before this book came along, but until now it was often possible to ignore the evidence. Now [liberals] are reduced to misrepresenting it, and to lashing out at the messengers."[4]

The most influential critique came from the American evolutionary biologist Stephen Jay Gould,* who said that the book's assumptions were fundamentally racist, insofar as they justify and legitimize existing racial disparities; by arguing that existing differences between racial groups are biologically determined, *The Bell Curve* suggests that racial minorities are responsible for their own underachievement. Moreover, he found the bases of the authors' findings to be unscientific, noting many problems with *The Bell Curve*'s analyses, including the authors' reliance on a single data set— the National Longitudinal Survey of Youth (NLSY)*—for the majority of their conclusions.[5]

Other critics have taken similar stances. A number of contributors to the volume *Intelligence, Genes, and Success* (1997) argue that Herrnstein and Murray overestimated the heritability* of intelligence.[6] The authors of *Inequality by Design: Cracking the Bell Curve Myth* (1996) reanalyzed the NLSY data, demonstrating that, when other variables are added to the equation, intelligence becomes a weaker predictor of life outcomes.[7] In other critiques, the argument is put forward that that environmental influences play as large a role as genes,* or a larger one.

Responses

Herrnstein died before *The Bell Curve* was published. As a result, the burden of responding to critics fell on Murray. One of the charges made against the book was that studying race* in biological terms was misguided (many social scientists* believe that race is a social construct) or unworthy of scholarly attention when addressing the root causes of poverty, crime, and other social ills. Murray responded vehemently, arguing that scholarly attitudes have failed to keep up with changes in modern genetics.*[8]

Murray does not mince words in addressing his critics. Reflecting on *The Bell Curve* 20 years after its publication, he argued: "[The] reaction to *The Bell Curve* exposed a profound corruption of the social sciences that has prevailed since the 1960s. *The Bell Curve* is a relentlessly moderate book—both in its use of evidence and in its tone—and yet it was excoriated [severely criticized] in remarkably personal and vicious ways, sometimes by eminent academicians who knew very well they were lying."[9]

Murray's most recent book, *Coming Apart: The State of White America, 1960–2010*,[10] continues to respond to charges of racism. Unlike *The Bell Curve*, *Coming Apart* focuses on class, not race. In the book, Murray criticizes two classes of white Americans: those from the isolated upper class, and those from the morally decaying lower class. He charges the upper class with living in a secluded bubble, and the lower class for perpetuating moral decay. Many critics interpreted *The Bell Curve* as an ideologically racist attack on minorities. But *Coming Apart* offers a comparably critical view of white citizens of the United States.

Conflict and Consensus

The intense debates over *The Bell Curve* have not helped the opponents in the argument to reach a consensus. In an interview conducted 20 years after the initial publication of *The Bell Curve*, Murray stood steadfastly by his theses. He cited two decades of subsequent data that show that the divide between people of different cognitive ability is continuing, if not accelerating. He argued that the data also show that gaps in IQ* and SAT* (Scholastic Aptitude Test) scores are not closing in any substantial way between racial groups.[11]

Supporters and critics of *The Bell Curve* largely talk past one another when they debate these matters. Part of the reason that the book remains important today, despite the fact that many of its claims have been questioned, is because *The Bell Curve* powerfully ignited a debate on the nature and origins of intelligence that continues today. Furthermore, the response to the book highlighted the fact that many of the historical and current ideas about intelligence may be politically motivated or biased in their nature.

Murray has not responded directly or extensively to specific critiques concerning the way data were analyzed in *The Bell Curve*. While this limits the seriousness with which the core arguments from the book are taken today, the overarching idea that there are differences in intelligence between different ethnic groups* remains a controversial and very complex question.

NOTES

1 Steven Fraser, ed., *The Bell Curve Wars: Race, Intelligence, and the Future of America* (New York: Basic Books, 1995); Russell Jacoby and Naomi Glauberman, eds., *The Bell Curve Debate: History, Documents, Opinion* (New York: Times Books, 1995).

2 Frank Miele, "For Whom the Bell Tolls: An Interview with the Author of *The Bell Curve*: Charles Murray," *Skeptic* 3 (1995): 34–41.

3 Bob Herbert, "In America; Throwing a Curve, *The New York Times*, October 26, 1994.

4 Daniel Seligman, "Trashing *The Bell Curve*," *The National Review* 46, no. 23 (1994), 60–1.

5 Stephen Jay Gould, "Curveball", *The New Yorker*, November 28, 1994.

6   Bernie Devlin, *Intelligence, Genes, and Success : Scientists Respond to
     The Bell Curve* (New York: Springer, 1997).

7   Claude S. Fischer, *Inequality by Design: Cracking the Bell Curve Myth*
     (Princeton, NJ: Princeton University Press, 1996).

8   Charles Murray, "Book Review, *A Troublesome Inheritance* by Nicholas
     Wade," *Wall Street Journal*, May 2, 2014.

9   "The Bell Curve 20 Years Later: A Q & A with Charles Murray" (https://www.
     aei.org/publication/bell-curve-20–years-later-qa-charles-murray/, accessed
     October 15, 2015).

10   Charles Murray, *Coming Apart: The State of White America 1960–2010*
     (New York: Random House, 2012).

11   "The Bell Curve 20 Years Later."

THE EVOLVING DEBATE

KEY POINTS

- Although there has been further progress in genetic*
  research, little work has since been done on the explicit
  conjunction of intelligence, race,* and inequality.

- Researchers in intelligence and social behavior continue to
  investigate the factor of genetic inheritance in their field.

- Although few subsequent publications have ignited a
  controversy as heated as those caused by *The Bell Curve*,
  debates about nature versus nurture* have continued in
  new forms.

Uses and Problems

The Bell Curve: Intelligence and Class Structure in American Life by
Richard J. Herrnstein and Charles Murray portrays America as divided
between an intellectual elite* and an intellectually challenged lower
class. The book had two key effects:

- It brought questions about the nature of intelligence—
  previously a debate found only in academic and philosophical
  circles—into the public and political spheres.

- It had a powerful influence on the evolution of the study
  of intelligence. *The Bell Curve* reignited the "nature versus
  nurture" debate between those who believe that intelligence
  is a genetically determined trait and those who believe it is
  strongly affected by nurture (that is, the environment).

Prior to *The Bell Curve*, the "nature" camp had been marginalized

> ❝ It seems likely that *The Bell Curve* will be one of the most written-about and talked-about works of social science* since the Kinsey Report* 50 years ago. ❞
> Charles Murray, "*The Bell Curve* and its Critics," *Commentary*

as discussions of racial differences in intelligence implied that certain races were inferior to others; this appeared to justify unequal treatment of racial groups based on such inferiority. Herrnstein and Murray's text challenged this state of affairs, putting discussions of racial differences in intelligence in the spotlight and provoking an already divided academic community.

Since the book's publication, however, the debate has become more nuanced, or less sharply divided. Today the opposition between heredity (genetic inheritance) and environment is being questioned.[1] A new generation of scholars has shown that genes* and the environment are not independent phenomena but, rather, interact in dynamic ways. In other words, nature and nurture do not involve separate spheres, as much of what is labeled "genetic" or "hereditary" becomes meaningful only in the context of the environment. The current consensus is that a large part of intelligence is indeed, as Herrnstein and Murray argued, genetically determined—but genes are only important for their ability to define the *limits* of intelligence; environment and experience determine if and when those limits will be reached.

Schools of Thought

How far can the arguments made by *The Bell Curve* be said to be universal? That question is as contested as the arguments themselves, and there are strong proponents and critics on both sides. This has led to many new studies on intelligence. Current findings suggest that, with regard to the nature versus nurture debate, the question is not whether nature or nurture is more important, but how nature and nurture interact and influence one another. Current research is focused on the search for specific gene variations associated with differences in intelligence; researchers are also looking at the environmental forces that can modify gene expression. These developments may be critical in furthering our future understanding of intelligence.

Critics of *The Bell Curve* have argued against Herrnstein and Murray's depiction of intelligence as a single, uniform entity. The American developmental psychologist* Howard Gardner,* for example, is a proponent of the theory of multiple intelligences.* He points out that what is considered "intelligent" is culturally bound, and that the idea of a unitary intellectual quotient is an exclusively Western idea.[2] Gardner, who argues that other cultures have vastly different ideas of intelligence, also writes, "Outside the closed world of [researchers who base their psychological analyses on statistical measurements] … a more empirically sensitive and scientifically compelling understanding of human intelligence has emerged in the past hundred years. Many authorities have challenged the notion of a single intelligence or even the concept of intelligence altogether."[3] Instead, such researchers focus on training, creativity, practice, and motivation, forms of intelligence that are not captured by IQ* tests.

In Current Scholarship

Although Herrnstein and Murray make no direct claims about the universality of their findings in *The Bell Curve*, a book published in 2008 builds on the premises it lays out. In *The Global Bell Curve: Race, IQ, and Inequality Worldwide*, the politically conservative* British psychology professor Richard Lynn* examines the extent to which Herrnstein and Murray's thesis holds for other societies. Lynn states that his book has "[examined] whether the theory advanced by Herrnstein and Murray in *The Bell Curve*—that race differences in intelligence go a long way to explain the differences in educational attainment, earnings, socioeconomic status, crime, longevity, infant mortality, fertility, and other social phenomena in the United States— holds for other multiracial societies. The results of this inquiry are a resounding confirmation of the thesis of *The Bell Curve*."[4]

Questions have been raised, however, over whether Lynn's arguments are politically motivated. He holds right-wing political views and receives funding for his scholarship from conservative think tanks.*[5]

The British author Nicholas Wade,* a former *New York Times* science reporter, has also substantiated many of the claims about the genetic heritability* of intelligence that are found in *The Bell Curve*. In his book of 2014, *A Troublesome Inheritance: Genes, Race, and Human History*, Wade marshals recent evidence in genetics* and evolutionary biology to claim that there are biological reasons for variance in specific traits between ethnic groups.*[6] Murray has praised Wade's book for challenging the "intellectual orthodoxy" that questions the important role of genetic inheritance.[7]

NOTES

1   Eric Turkheimer *et al.*, "Socioeconomic Status Modifies Heritability of IQ in Young Children," *Psychological Science* 4 (2003): 623–8.

2   Steven Fraser, *The Bell Curve Wars: Race, Intelligence, and the Future of America* (New York: Basic Books, 2006), 23–35.

3   Howard Gardner, "Cracking the IQ Box," *The American Prospect*, December 10, 2001 (http://prospect.org/article/cracking-open-iq-box, accessed October 30, 2015).

4   Richard Lynn, *The Global Bell Curve: Race, IQ, and Inequality Worldwide* (Washington, DC: Washington Summit Publishers, 2006), 289.

5   Leon Kamin, "Behind the Curve," *Scientific American* (February 1995): 99–102.

6   Nicholas Wade, *A Troublesome Inheritance: Genes, Race, and Human History* (New York: Penguin, 2014).

7   Charles Murray, "Book Review, *A Troublesome Inheritance* by Nicholas Wade," *The Wall Street Journal*, May 2, 2014.

IMPACT AND INFLUENCE TODAY

KEY POINTS

- More than three decades after its initial publication, *The Bell Curve* remains central to debates about genetic* differences and social policy.

- The persistence of inequality, and its overwhelmingly racial character in the United States, continues to pose a provocative challenge to scholars and policy-makers.

- Current work in behavioral genetics* (the study of the interplay between genes* and the environment) is developing themes that are present in *The Bell Curve*.

Position

If Richard J. Herrnstein and Charles Murray's *The Bell Curve: Intelligence and Class Structure in American Life* is still a relevant text, it is largely because the question of intelligence remains an open and contentious debate. Herrnstein and Murray's critics argue that intelligence is not a unitary, hereditary*(genetically inherited) construct. But books have also been published that reiterate and provide additional evidence for the major points made in *The Bell Curve*; in 1998, for example, the American education psychologist Arthur Jensen*published *The g Factor: The Science of Mental Ability*. In it Jensen, a long-standing proponent of the hereditary view of intelligence, summarizes an extensive array of studies on the nature of intelligence. He provides evidence for the existence of general intelligence, g*—a construct that is central to the arguments of *The Bell Curve*.[1] Jensen shows that intelligence test scores predict a multitude of measures of information-processing efficiency. He also shows that intelligence, as measured by IQ* tests, itself holds many

> **❝** Murray and Herrnstein have written a book that deals with extraordinarily important issues, many of which have been considered too explosive to discuss in the public arena yet need to be aired. **❞**
>
> Richard Nesbitt, "Blue Genes," *The New Republic*

direct biological correlates.

In *The Bell Curve*, Herrnstein and Murray focus on genes alone. But in recent years, research has focused on gene–environment interactions—how the genetic traits passed down by one's parents are shaped by features of the social environment. These new findings show that genes and the environment are not independent phenomena that involve separate spheres, but, rather, are a matter of interaction— the way genes influence behavior largely depends on the environmental context in which those genes find themselves.[2] In light of this new research, it seems that Herrnstein and Murray's exclusive focus on genes alone may have been misplaced.

Interaction

The intensity of the critiques issued in response to *The Bell Curve* have had an effect on the way its ideas have been explored. New researchers have been reluctant to publicly discuss the policy implications of the idea that intelligence is heritable.* As a result, the usefulness of the text as an inspiration for politically libertarian* policy recommendations, which call for an end to such things as government welfare* programs, has been diminished. The most forceful critiques take exception to the idea that disadvantaged racial minorities are responsible for their life outcomes, so efforts to assist them are futile.

However, questions about general intelligence, g, continue to be a topic of empirical inquiry. In a recent article, two UK-based academics, Robert Plomin,* Professor of Behavioural Genetics at King's College London,* and Ian Deary,* Professor of Psychology at the University of Edinburgh,* claim that intelligence is a key predictor of life outcomes. For them, intelligence is "a core construct in differential psychology* and behavioral genetics,* and should be so in cognitive neuroscience.* It is one of the best predictors of important life outcomes such as education, occupation, mental and physical health and illness, and mortality."[3]

Although the debate over whether IQ* has a genetic or an environmental basis continues within academic circles, public interest in the issue has diminished. Instead, several high-profile killings of unarmed black men by police[4] have concentrated public attention in another direction. Rather than thinking about genetic differences between black people and white people, public interest is now focused on how these communities interact differently with the criminal justice system.

The Continuing Debate

The Bell Curve is viewed in two distinct ways, depending on the observer's political affiliations. While conservatives* regard the book as an instance of scholarship upending political orthodoxies, liberals* see it as an unfortunate popularization of scientific racism.* Given this polarization of opinion, a consensus on the political themes of the book is unlikely to be reached in the near future. Questions of social welfare* and affirmative action* continue to be contested political issues. Many disciples of the anti-welfare, anti–affirmative action position that is delineated clearly in *The Bell Curve* continue to champion this cause.

The Bell Curve is not remembered for its ideas alone. These days it is remembered, primarily, as an artifact of the "culture wars"* that were waged in America during the 1980s and 1990s. In 2015 the American historian Andrew Hartman* noted the speed with which challenges were made to the science behind *The Bell Curve*—but noted also that following the book's publication an argument was commonly "put forward by some liberals and many conservatives that even if *The Bell Curve*'s social science* was wrong, its political instincts were right."[5] It is likely that future debates about race* and inequality will feature modified versions of Herrnstein and Murray's core themes.

NOTES

1 Arthur Jensen, *The g Factor: The Science of Mental Ability* (Westport, CT: Greenwood Publishing, 1998).

2 Robert Plomin and Frank Spinath, "Intelligence: Genetics, Genes, and Genomics," *Journal of Personality and Social Psychology* 86 (2004): 112–29.

3 Robert Plomin and Ian Dreary, "Genetics and Intelligence Differences: Five Special Findings, *Molecular Psychiatry* 20 (2015): 98–108.

4 Claudia Rankine, "The Condition of Black Life is One of Mourning," *New York Times Magazine*, June 22, 2015 (http://www.nytimes.com/2015/06/22/magazine/the-condition-of-black-life-is-one-of-mourning.html, accessed October 15, 2015).

5 Andrew Hartman, *A War for the Soul of America: A History of the Culture Wars* (Chicago: University of Chicago Press, 2015), 119.

WHERE NEXT?

KEY POINTS

- *The Bell Curve* will likely remain in the public consciousness as a remnant of the culture wars* rather than as a substantive contribution to scholarly debates over intelligence and social policy.

- The specific findings of *The Bell Curve* are less relevant to current scholarship than the book's themes.

- *The Bell Curve* is one of the twentieth century's most significant works of social science* because of the controversy it provoked rather than because of its scholarly contribution.

Potential

When Richard J. Herrnstein and Charles Murray published *The Bell Curve: Intelligence and Class Structure in American Life* in 1994, they revived a debate over the nature and origins of intelligence, race,* and the future of the United States that is still ongoing. While the authors were not the first to argue for a biological basis for intelligence, their narrative was innovative in presenting variations in cognitive ability* as a far-reaching, comprehensive explanation for society's worst ills—poverty, crime, underachievement, joblessness, and child illegitimacy.*[1] Theirs is an account of how the divided state of the United States in the twentieth century can be explained by the intelligence of its citizens. While an intellectual elite* gains access to the best colleges and occupations, an intellectually impoverished underclass is consigned to underachievement.

While the corrosive effects of inequality still feature prominently in public debate, discussion now focuses largely on economics. In

> ❝The twentieth century dawned on a world segregated into social classes* defined in terms of money, power, and status. The ancient lines of separation based on hereditary rank were being erased, replaced by a more complicated set of overlapping lines. Social standing still played a major role, if less often accompanied by a sword or tiara, but so did out-and-out wealth, educational credentials, and, increasingly, talent. ❞
>
> Richard J. Herrnstein and Charles Murray, *The Bell Curve: Intelligence and Class Structure in American Life*

recent years, wealth disparities across all groups have grown to levels not seen since the catastrophic economic downturn of the 1920s and 1930s known as the Great Depression.*[2] Herrnstein and Murray's attempts to bring race and the heritable* trait of intelligence into these debates are no longer widely accepted. Mainstream discussions of race have moved on. In the wake of several high-profile killings of unarmed black men by police officers, the current focus of discussion on race centers on race and justice. In *Between the World and Me,* the prominent African American journalist Ta-Nehisi Coates* writes in a letter to his 15-year-old son, "… and you know now, if you did not before, that the police departments of your country have been endowed with the authority to destroy your body."[3] The timeliness of the book helped to make it a national bestseller, selling over 175,000 copies within the first month of its publication.[4]

Future Directions

In his book of 2012, *Coming Apart: The State of White America 1960–2010*, Charles Murray has continued his focus on class stratification and its long-term effects.[5] The same issues of class divisions and race that prompted the writing of *The Bell Curve* continue to challenge contemporary American society. In this sense, some of the book's concerns remain in the mainstream of political and scholarly thinking.

In fact, some of Murray's concerns are shared by the American political scientist*Robert Putnam,* the author of a widely discussed work of social science, *Bowling Alone* (2000). *Bowling Alone* talks about the importance of social capital* (that is, the value inherent in the network of relationships between people living within a society). He sees this as vital for achieving success in life.[6] Putnam's book *Our Kids: The American Dream in Crisis* (2015) shares some of *The Bell Curve*'s preoccupations with class stratification.[7] While Putnam is a liberal* and does not share Murray's libertarian* politics, he has written that "Charles Murray's portrait … of America's coming apart is … largely accurate, as far as it goes"[8]—but goes on to emphasize that "this split is about class and not about race." His remark shows that if *The Bell Curve* is going to continue to have an impact on public debates, these will be debates about inequality and not about race.

Summary

Herrnstein and Murray's book *The Bell Curve* was aptly named. A bell curve is an established mathematical term that describes the nature of populations—it is an inverse U-shaped distribution where the majority of data points are in the middle (i.e. "average"), and few data points are at the high or low extremes. In choosing this title (at the suggestion of their editor), Herrnstein and Murray captured the essence of their argument—that differences between groups in America can be explained by scientific realities about the nature of genes* and the nature of intelligence. The title serves as a visual illustration of the society the authors portray: at one end is a small, select group of elite* individuals defined by their high intelligence; at the other end is a group of impoverished individuals defined by their low intelligence. Herrnstein and Murray's thesis that these differences reflect inborn racial divides in America was explosive at the time when

The Bell Curve was published, and it remains explosive today.

The Bell Curve's impact on politics and policy will change as the political climate changes. How political and public opinion will shift on the issues it highlights remains an open question; much of what happens among American government officials and policy-makers today depends on the influence of "policy entrepreneurs"*— individuals with academic backgrounds who sponsor specific intellectual traditions and promote specific policy solutions.[9] While economics, rather than biology, is today seen as the basis for class stratification, the status of *The Bell Curve* as one of the most explosive works of social science to have been produced in the twentieth century is secure.

NOTES

1 Arthur Jensen, "How Much Can We Boost IQ and Scholastic Achievement?" *Harvard Educational Review* 39 (1969): 1–123.

2 Thomas Piketty, *Capital in the 21st Century* (Boston: Belknap Press, 2014).

3 Ta-Nehisi Coates, *Between the World and Me* (New York: Spiegel & Grau, 2015).

4 Jocelyn McClurg, "Ta-Nehisi Coates Writes a Best Seller," *USA Today,* July 22, 2015 (http://www.usatoday.com/story/life/books/2015/07/22/ta-nehisi-coates-between-world-and-me-harper-lee-el-james-usa-today-best-selling-books/30471757/, accessed October 15, 2015).

5 Charles Murray, *Coming Apart: The State of White America 1960–2010* (New York: Random House, 2012).

6 Robert D. Putnam, *Bowling Alone: The Collapse and Revival of American Community* (New York: Simon & Schuster, 2000).

7 Robert D. Putnam, *Our Kids: The American Dream in Crisis* (New York: Simon & Schuster, 2015).

8 http://www.aspenideas.org/session/are-we-really-coming-apart, accessed October 31, 2015.

9 See Martin Rein and Christopher Winship, *Policy Entrepreneurs and the Academic Establishment: Truth and Values in Social Controversies* (Cambridge, MA: Harvard University Press, 1997).

GLOSSARY

GLOSSARY OF TERMS

Affirmative action: policies that increase the representation of women and minorities in education, employment, and other areas where they have been historically underrepresented.

American Dream: a belief that hard work will lead to success in life. It is a version of achievement ideology, which holds that our capacity to succeed is largely a function of individual effort.

American Enterprise Institute: a privately funded think tank located in Washington, DC that advocates for conservative causes.

American Institutes for Research: a nonprofit, nonpartisan social science research organization that conducts studies on issues such as education, health, and international development.

Behavioral genetics: a modern science that studies the interplay between genetic and environmental factors in explaining differences between individuals.

City College of New York: a public university located in New York City.

Civil Rights Act of 1964: a sweeping law that prevented discrimination based on race, color, religion, sex, or national origin. As a result, racial segregation in schools ended and the voting rights of minorities were protected.

Civil society: nongovernmental voluntary organizations of citizens. Civil society is also distinct from the concerns of business.

Class: the grouping of individuals in a society, traditionally according to shared economic characteristics.

Cognitive ability: another term for IQ and intelligence in *The Bell Curve*.

Cognitive class: a term that refers to the sorting of society. Generally society is sorted by economic class (commonly upper class, middle class, working class), but Herrnstein and Murray suggest that class should instead be understood as a function of cognitive ability.

Cognitive elite: a term used by Herrnstein and Murray to describe intelligent people who graduate from the most prestigious colleges and work in the most prestigious occupations.

Cognitive neuroscience: the study of mental processes by investigating the nature of the brain.

Cognitive partitioning: the isolation of cognitive classes from one another in educational and employment settings.

Conservative: politically, someone who believes in the power of markets over governments and favors tradition over radical changes in society.

Culture wars: a series of high-profile debates in the 1980s and 1990s that pitted liberals against conservatives on issues such as abortion, affirmative action, welfare reform, gay marriage, evolution, censorship, and educational standards.

Developmental psychology: a branch of psychology that studies changes in mental life over time.

Differential psychology: a branch of psychology involved with differences between both individuals and groups of individuals.

Dysgenic Pressure: the gradual reduction of IQ in a population due to changes in the gene pool.

Educational psychology: a branch of psychology that studies mental and emotional development among children and young adults, especially as this pertains to learning outcomes.

Elite: those at the uppermost levels of the class structure, defined by high levels of wealth, important occupations, and high educational achievement levels.

Enlightenment: the term given to a seventeenth- and eighteenth-century European intellectual movement that championed the individual use of reason over deference to authorities like the Church.

Ethnic groups: Herrnstein and Murray prefer "ethnic group" to "race" because of the difficulties in defining race. The ethnic groups they study are Latinos, blacks, whites (that is, non-Latino whites), and Asians, and all categories are based on the self-identification of participants in the data they used in their study.

Eugenics: the attempt to promote or reduce traits within a population through selective breeding or sterilization.

Evolution: the process by which the inherited characteristics of populations are altered over successive generations.

Experimental psychology: a branch of psychology that uses empirical methods (that is, it employs experiments designed to produce evidence that can be verified by observation) to the study of the human mind and behavior.

g (general intelligence): a statistical summary of the correlations between different measures of cognitive ability. IQ, in contrast, also measures mental ability but is based on performance on a (single) IQ test.

Genes: the material passed down from parents to children through DNA, a molecule that is the carrier of genetic information.

Genetic: a description of traits that are inherent and inheritable.

Genetic determinism: genetically determined traits are those passed down from parents to offspring. The term also refers to a belief that genes determine social behavior.

Genetics: the study of genes and their influence on health and behavior.

Gifted and talented programs: special accelerated educational programs for students who demonstrate very high achievement levels at an early age.

Great Depression: a period of prolonged economic hardship in the 1920s and 1930s in the United States. It was preceded by a period of extreme disparity in wealth.

Great Society programs: a set of federally funded, domestic programs aiming to reduce poverty and racial tension in the United States. They were introduced in President Lyndon Baines Johnson's inaugural address in 1965.

H1–B Visa program: a program granting foreign workers the right to work in the United States. Its aim is to attract talented foreign workers to skilled positions.

Harvard University: an elite private university located in Cambridge, Massachusetts.

Hereditary: a term referring to traits that are genetically inherited.

Heritability: this term is used interchangeably with "genetics"; both refer to traits that are passed from parents to offspring.

Illegitimacy: children born to unmarried parents.

IQ: intelligence quotient, a quantifiable way of measuring individual differences in intelligence, as determined by tests.

King's College London: a public research university located in London, England.

Kinsey Reports: a set of studies on human sexuality published in 1948 and 1953 that generated great controversy.

Liberalism: a world view that centers on equality and liberty.

Libertarian: a political ideology that champions a radical form of individual freedom and greatly resists government-run programs.

Manhattan Institute for Policy Research: a right-wing think tank founded in 1978 in New York City by Antony Fisher and William J. Casey.

Massachusetts Institute of Technology: an elite American research university located in Cambridge, Massachusetts. While it is best known for programs in science and engineering, it also has strong departments in the social sciences and humanities.

Meritocracy: a system in which advancement is based solely on ability and achievement (that is, merit).

Minority groups: racial and ethnic groups that comprise the minority of the population and that are often underrepresented in positions of power. In the United States, the primary minority groups are African Americans, Latinos, and Asian Americans.

Moynihan Report (1965): formally titled "The Negro Family: The Case for National Action," this is a report by sociologist Daniel Patrick Moynihan about problems of poverty, illegitimacy, and crime in African American communities.

Multiculturalism: the existence of several cultures inside a territory. Proponents of multiculturalism in education advocate the presentation of perspectives from multiple traditions, especially those of minority cultures.

Multiple intelligences: a theory of intelligence championed by the psychologist Howard Gardner. It holds that intelligence is not unitary, but expresses itself in several different forms. Gardner originally looked at musical–rhythmic, visual–spatial, verbal–linguistic, logical–mathematical, bodily–kinesthetic, interpersonal, intrapersonal, and naturalistic intelligence. He later added existential and moral intelligence.

Nature versus nurture: the debate over whether an individual's life outcomes are a product of their innate, biologically determined qualities (that is, nature) as opposed to their environment and experiences (that is, nurture).

Nazi: the National Socialist German Workers' Party that came to power under Adolf Hitler in 1933.

New Deal: a raft of government-funded employment and social welfare programs in the 1930s to help the United States emerge from the economic downturn known as the Great Depression. They were passed during the presidency of Franklin Delano Roosevelt.

NLSY: the National Longitudinal Survey of Youth was a study carried out by the Bureau of Labor Statistics that began collecting substantial information on unemployment among a generation of young people beginning in 1979.

Permanent underclass: a theory that one group will occupy the lowest ranks of social hierarchies for generations with little chance of advancement.

Policy entrepreneurship: the phenomenon whereby individuals with academic backgrounds sponsor specific political policies and attempt to change public policy.

Political science: the study of political behavior and systems of government.

Political taboo: a topic generally avoided in political discourse.

Pseudo-science: a belief that claims to be based on the scientific method, but fails the test of rigorous scientific scrutiny.

Psychology: the study of the human mind and behavior.

Race: social categories commonly used to distinguish whites, blacks, Asians, and so on. Here, the problem of race refers to the different life outcomes experienced by these social groups and how to explain such differences. Throughout *The Bell Curve* Herrnstein and Murray prefer the term "ethnic group" to "race."

Regression analysis: a statistical method for considering the relationship between many variables. *The Bell Curve* uses regression analysis to argue that intelligence is a better predictor of social behavior than socioeconomic status.

Remedial education: programs for underperforming, often low-income students.

SAT: the Scholastic Aptitude Test is a standardized test measuring verbal and mathematical ability taken by high school students. It is an important factor in college admission decisions.

Scientific racism: the use of scientific methods to substantiate the belief that some racial groups are superior to others and that these differences justify unequal treatment of groups.

Social capital: connections between individuals, and the common civic values that influence a society, and the nature, extent, and impact of these.

Social Darwinism: the application of Charles Darwin's notion of "survival of the fittest" to human society. Often used to justify existing hierarchies in society.

Social hierarchies: differences between individuals and groups in income, educational achievement, employment, and other indicators of power and success.

Social inequality: a term expressing great differences between those at the top and bottom of the social hierarchy.

Social science: the academic study of human beings and social groups. It includes the disciplines of anthropology, economics, geography, history, political science, psychology, social studies, and sociology.

Socioeconomic status: a common class indicator which takes into account both economic status and social position, including gender, race, and family history.

Sociology: the study of the development, structure, and functioning of society.

Stanford–Binet test: a common intelligence test to measure knowledge, quantitative reasoning, visual–spatial processing, working memory, and fluid reasoning in individuals.

Statistically significant: a set of data large enough to suggest a correlation between a variable and a measured phenomenon.

Supreme Court: the highest court in the United States.

The National Review: a conservative magazine founded in the United States in 1955.

The New Republic: a generally liberal magazine founded in the United States in 1912.

Think tank: a privately funded organization that conducts research and advocates for policy changes.

Underclass: the lowest levels of the class structure, defined by poverty, low employment levels, and high crime rates.

University of Edinburgh: a public research university located in Edinburgh, Scotland.

War on Poverty: the name given to legislation introduced by President Lyndon Baines Johnson in his 1964 State of the Union address. Part of his "Great Society" programs, the War on Poverty greatly increased the role of the federal government in education, housing, welfare, and healthcare in low-income communities.

Welfare Reform program: officially called "The Personal Responsibility and Work Opportunity Act," this 1996 legislation radically reduced social welfare programs for single mothers. Bill Clinton attributed many of the ideas behind the reform to Charles Murray.

Welfare: state-sponsored assistance programs for the poor and underprivileged.

World War II: a global war from 1939 to 1945 centered in Europe and the Pacific. It was fought between the Allies, led by Great Britain, France, the US and the Soviet Union, and the Axis, led by Nazi Germany.

PEOPLE MENTIONED IN THE TEXT

Edmund Burke (1729–1797) was an Anglo-Irish politician and social critic who in 1790 published *Reflections on the Revolution in France*. The pamphlet, a best seller at the time, questioned the swiftness and violence of the French Revolution and advocated for a more gradual form of social progress that respected the traditions developed within national cultures as opposed to universal human rights.

Bill Clinton (b. 1946) was the 42nd president of the United States, in office from 1993 to 2001. He is a Democrat.

Ta-Nehisi Coates (b. 1975) is a prominent African American journalist and social critic. He frequently writes about issues of race and politics.

Charles Darwin (1809–1882) is best known for his evolution research and coining of the term "natural selection," which refers to the way in which nature selects for adaptive characteristics in animals over time.

Ian Deary (b. 1954) is a Scottish psychologist best known for his research on intelligence. He is professor of differential psychology at The University of Edinburgh.

Sir Francis Galton (1822–1911) was an English anthropologist, explorer, and statistician. The cousin of Charles Darwin, he was an early supporter of the theory of evolution.

Howard Gardner (b. 1943) is an American developmental psychologist at Harvard University best known for the idea that there are multiple forms of intelligence.

Stephen Jay Gould (1941–2002) was an American paleontologist and evolutionary biologist. Aside from his scholarly writing he wrote many works for a general audience.

Andrew Hartman is an intellectual historian at Illinois State University and a prominent liberal social critic.

Bob Herbert (b. 1945) was a columnist for the *New York Times* newspaper.

Frederick Hess (b. 1967) is a conservative political scientist and fellow at the American Enterprise Institute.

Oliver Wendell Holmes, Jr (1841–1935) was an Associate Justice of the Supreme Court from 1902 to 1935.

Christopher Jencks (b. 1936) is an American social scientist at Harvard University's Kennedy School of Government.

Arthur Jensen (1923–2012) was an American educational psychologist most famous for his work on how genetics contributed to intelligence and personality.

Lyndon Baines Johnson (1908–1973) was the 36th president of the United States, in office from 1963 to 1969. He was a Democrat.

Richard Lynn (b. 1930) is a British psychologist best known for his work on racial differences in intelligence.

Frank Miele (b. 1948) is a journalist and editor of the *Skeptic* magazine.

Daniel Patrick Moynihan (1927–2003) was an American sociologist and politician. He was a four-term senator from New York State.

Richard Nisbett (b. 1941) is a social psychologist at the University of Michigan.

Michael Novak (b. 1933) is a conservative intellectual and frequent contributor to the *National Review*.

Karl Pearson (1857–1936) was an English mathematician and statistician.

Robert Plomin (b. 1948) is an American behavioral geneticist best known for studies involving twins.

Robert Putnam (b. 1941) is an influential American sociologist at Harvard University. He is the author of *Bowling Alone*, a best-selling book on the importance of social capital for achieving success.

Ronald Reagan (1911–2004) was the 40th president of the United States, in office from 1981 to 1989. He was a Republican.

Daniel Seligman (1924–2009) was an editor at *Fortune* magazine.

B. F. Skinner (1904–1990) was an American psychologist. He was a founder of behaviorism, a theory that said human action was conditioned by rewards and punishments.

Charles Spearman (1863–1945) was an English psychologist best known for work in statistics and his theory of general intelligence, the g factor.

Nicholas Wade (b. 1942) is an English science reporter who formerly wrote for the *New York Times*.

William Julius Wilson (b. 1935) is an American sociologist at Harvard University whose work deals with race in America.

WORKS CITED

WORKS CITED

Baum, Richard. "Richard J. Herrnstein: A Memoir." *Behavioral Analysis* 17 (1994): 201–6.

Berger, Brigitte. "Methodological Fetishism." *The National Review* 46 (1994): 54.

Capron, Christiane, and Michel Duyme. "Assessment of Effects of Socio-economic Status on IQ in a Full Cross-fostering Study." *Nature* 340 (1989): 552–4.

Coates, Ta-Nehisi. *Between the World and Me*. New York: Spiegel & Grau, 2015.

Devlin, Bernie. *Intelligence, Genes, and Success: Scientists Respond to* The Bell Curve New York: Springer, 1997.

Fischer, Claude S. *Inequality by Design: Cracking the Bell Curve Myth*. Princeton, NJ: Princeton University Press, 1996.

Fletcher, Richard, and John Hattie. *Intelligence and Intelligence Testing*. New York: Routledge, 2011.

Fraser, Stephen, ed. *The Bell Curve Wars: Race, Intelligence, and the Future of America*. New York: Basic Books, 2006.

Galton, Francis. *Hereditary Genius.* London: Macmillan, 1982.

Gardner, Howard. "Cracking the IQ Box." *The American Prospect*, December 10, 2001 (http://prospect.org/article/cracking-open-iq-box, accessed October 30, 2015).

———. *Frames of Mind: The Theory of Multiple Intelligences*. New York: Basic Books, 1983.

Goleman, Daniel. "Richard Herrnstein, 64, Dies; Backed Nature Over Nurture." *The New York Times*, September 16, 1994.

Gould, Stephen J. *The Mismeasure of Man*. New York: W. W. Norton, 1981.

Guttman, Amy. *Multiculturalism: Examining the Politics of Recognition*. Princeton, NJ: Princeton University Press, 1994.

Hartman, Andrew. *A War for the Soul of America: A History of the Culture Wars*. Chicago: University of Chicago Press, 2015.

Herbert, Bob. "In America; Throwing a Curve." *New York Times* October 26, 1994.

Herrnstein, Richard J. "IQ," *The Atlantic Monthly* 228 (1971): 43–64.

———. *IQ in the Meritocracy*. Boston: Little, Brown, 1973.

———. "On Challenging an Orthodoxy." *Commentary*, April 1, 1973.

Herrnstein, Richard J., and Charles A. Murray. *The Bell Curve: Intelligence and Class Structure in American Life*. New York: Basic Books, 1994.

Hess, Frederick. "America's Future Depends on Gifted and Talented Students." *The New York Times*, June 4, 2014.

Jacoby, Russell, and Naomi Glauberman, eds. *The Bell Curve Debate: History, Documents, Opinions*. New York: Random House, 1995.

Jencks, Christopher, Marshall Smith, Henry Acland, Mary Jo Bane, David Cohen, Herbert Gintis, Barbara Heyns, and Stephan Michelson. *Inequality: A Reassessment of the Effect of Family and Schooling in America*. New York: Basic Books, 1972.

Jensen, Arthur. *The g Factor: The Science of Mental Ability*. Westport, CT: Greenwood Publishing, 1998.

———. "How Much Can We Boost IQ and Scholastic Achievement?" *Harvard Educational Review* 39 (1969): 1–123.

Kamin, Leon. "Behind the Curve." *Scientific American*, February 1995: 99–102.

Lynn, Richard. *The Global Bell Curve: Race, IQ and Inequality Worldwide*. August, GA: Washington Summit Publishers, 1997.

McClurg, Jocelyn. "Ta-Nehisi Coates Writes a Best Seller." *USA Today,* July 22, 2015 (http://www.usatoday.com/story/life/books/2015/07/22/ta-nehisi-coates-between-world-and-me-harper-lee-el-james-usa-today-best-selling-books/30471757/, accessed October 15, 2015).

Miele, Frank. "For Whom the Bell Tolls: An Interview with the Author of *The Bell Curve*: Charles Murray." *Skeptic* 3 (1995): 34–41.

Murray, Charles A. "*The Bell Curve* and its Critics," *Commentary*, May 1, 1995.

———. "Book Review, *A Troublesome Inheritance* by Nicholas Wade." *The Wall Street Journal*, May 2, 2014.

———. *By the People: Rebuilding Liberty Without Permission*. New York: Crown Forum, 2015.

———. *Coming Apart: The State of White America 1960–2010*. New York: Random House, 2012.

———. *Losing Ground: American Social Policy, 1950–1980*. New York: Basic Books, 1984.

———. *What It Means to Be a Libertarian*. New York: Broadway Books, 1997. Murray, Charles, and Catherine Bly Cox. *Apollo: The Race to the Moon*. New York: Touchstone Books, 1989.

Nisbett, Richard. "Blue Genes." *The New Republic*, October 31, 1994 (http://

www.newrepublic.com/article/120890/tnr-staffers-and-others-respond-claims-bell-curve, accessed October 15, 2015).

Novak, Michael. "Sins of the Cognitive Elite," *The National Review* 46 (1994): 54–6.

Piketty, Thomas. *Capital in the 21st Century.* Boston: Belknap Press, 2014.

Plomin, Robert, and Ian Deary. "Genetics and Intelligence Differences: Five Special Findings." *Social Pscyhiatry* 20 (2015): 98–108.

Plomin, Robert, and Frank Spinath. "Intelligence: Genetics, Genes, and Genomics." *Journal of Personality and Social Psychology* 86 (2004): 112–29.

Preston, Julia. "Pink Slips at Disney. But First, Training Foreign Replacements," *New York* Times, June 3, 2015 (http://www.nytimes.com/2015/06/04/us/last-task-after-layoff-at-disney-train-foreign-replacements.html, accessed October 15, 2015).

Putnam, Robert D. *Bowling Alone: The Collapse and Revival of American Community.* New York: Simon & Schuster, 2000.

— — —. *Our Kids: The American Dream in Crisis.* New York: Simon & Schuster, 2015.

Rankine, Claudia. "The Condition of Black Life is One of Mourning." *New York Times Magazine*, June 22, 2015.

Rein, Martin, and Christopher Winship. *Policy Entrepreneurs and the Academic Establishment: Truth and Values in Social Controversies.* Cambridge, MA: Harvard University Press, 1997.

Seligman, Daniel. "Trashing *The Bell Curve.*" *National Review* 46, no. 23 (1994): 60–1.

Spearman, Charles. "General Intelligence, Objectively Determined and Measured." *American Journal of Psychology* 15 (1904): 201–29.

Turkheimer, Eric, Andreana Haley, Mary Waldron, Brian D'Onofrio, and Irving I. Gottesman. "Socioeconomic Status Modifies Heritability of IQ in Young Children." *Psychological Science* 4 (2003): 623–8.

Wade, Nicholas. *A Troublesome Inheritance: Genes, Race, and Human History.* New York: Penguin, 2014.

Watson, James. "Psychology as a Behaviorist Views It." *Psychological Review* 20 (1913): 158–77.

Wilson, James Q., and Richard J. *Herrnstein. Crime and Human Nature.* New York: Simon and Schuster, 1985.

THE MACAT LIBRARY
BY DISCIPLINE

AFRICANA STUDIES

Chinua Achebe's *An Image of Africa: Racism in Conrad's Heart of Darkness*
W. E. B. Du Bois's *The Souls of Black Folk*
Zora Neale Huston's *Characteristics of Negro Expression*
Martin Luther King Jr's *Why We Can't Wait*
Toni Morrison's *Playing in the Dark: Whiteness in the American Literary Imagination*

ANTHROPOLOGY

Arjun Appadurai's *Modernity at Large: Cultural Dimensions of Globalisation*
Philippe Ariès's *Centuries of Childhood*
Franz Boas's *Race, Language and Culture*
Kim Chan & Renée Mauborgne's *Blue Ocean Strategy*
Jared Diamond's *Guns, Germs & Steel: the Fate of Human Societies*
Jared Diamond's *Collapse: How Societies Choose to Fail or Survive*
E. E. Evans-Pritchard's *Witchcraft, Oracles and Magic Among the Azande*
James Ferguson's *The Anti-Politics Machine*
Clifford Geertz's *The Interpretation of Cultures*
David Graeber's *Debt: the First 5000 Years*
Karen Ho's *Liquidated: An Ethnography of Wall Street*
Geert Hofstede's *Culture's Consequences: Comparing Values, Behaviors, Institutes and Organizations across Nations*
Claude Lévi-Strauss's *Structural Anthropology*
Jay Macleod's *Ain't No Makin' It: Aspirations and Attainment in a Low-Income Neighborhood*
Saba Mahmood's *The Politics of Piety: The Islamic Revival and the Feminist Subject*
Marcel Mauss's *The Gift*

BUSINESS

Jean Lave & Etienne Wenger's *Situated Learning*
Theodore Levitt's *Marketing Myopia*
Burton G. Malkiel's *A Random Walk Down Wall Street*
Douglas McGregor's *The Human Side of Enterprise*
Michael Porter's *Competitive Strategy: Creating and Sustaining Superior Performance*
John Kotter's *Leading Change*
C. K. Prahalad & Gary Hamel's *The Core Competence of the Corporation*

CRIMINOLOGY

Michelle Alexander's *The New Jim Crow: Mass Incarceration in the Age of Colorblindness*
Michael R. Gottfredson & Travis Hirschi's *A General Theory of Crime*
Richard Herrnstein & Charles A. Murray's *The Bell Curve: Intelligence and Class Structure in American Life*
Elizabeth Loftus's *Eyewitness Testimony*
Jay Macleod's *Ain't No Makin' It: Aspirations and Attainment in a Low-Income Neighborhood*
Philip Zimbardo's *The Lucifer Effect*

ECONOMICS

Janet Abu-Lughod's *Before European Hegemony*
Ha-Joon Chang's *Kicking Away the Ladder*
David Brion Davis's *The Problem of Slavery in the Age of Revolution*
Milton Friedman's *The Role of Monetary Policy*
Milton Friedman's *Capitalism and Freedom*
David Graeber's *Debt: the First 5000 Years*
Friedrich Hayek's *The Road to Serfdom*
Karen Ho's *Liquidated: An Ethnography of Wall Street*

John Maynard Keynes's *The General Theory of Employment, Interest and Money*
Charles P. Kindleberger's *Manias, Panics and Crashes*
Robert Lucas's *Why Doesn't Capital Flow from Rich to Poor Countries?*
Burton G. Malkiel's *A Random Walk Down Wall Street*
Thomas Robert Malthus's *An Essay on the Principle of Population*
Karl Marx's *Capital*
Thomas Piketty's *Capital in the Twenty-First Century*
Amartya Sen's *Development as Freedom*
Adam Smith's *The Wealth of Nations*
Nassim Nicholas Taleb's *The Black Swan: The Impact of the Highly Improbable*
Amos Tversky's & Daniel Kahneman's *Judgment under Uncertainty: Heuristics and Biases*
Mahbub Ul Haq's *Reflections on Human Development*
Max Weber's *The Protestant Ethic and the Spirit of Capitalism*

FEMINISM AND GENDER STUDIES

Judith Butler's *Gender Trouble*
Simone De Beauvoir's *The Second Sex*
Michel Foucault's *History of Sexuality*
Betty Friedan's *The Feminine Mystique*
Saba Mahmood's *The Politics of Piety: The Islamic Revival and the Feminist Subject*
Joan Wallach Scott's *Gender and the Politics of History*
Mary Wollstonecraft's *A Vindication of the Rights of Woman*
Virginia Woolf's *A Room of One's Own*

GEOGRAPHY

The Brundtland Report's *Our Common Future*
Rachel Carson's *Silent Spring*
Charles Darwin's *On the Origin of Species*
James Ferguson's *The Anti-Politics Machine*
Jane Jacobs's *The Death and Life of Great American Cities*
James Lovelock's *Gaia: A New Look at Life on Earth*
Amartya Sen's *Development as Freedom*
Mathis Wackernagel & William Rees's *Our Ecological Footprint*

HISTORY

Janet Abu-Lughod's *Before European Hegemony*
Benedict Anderson's *Imagined Communities*
Bernard Bailyn's *The Ideological Origins of the American Revolution*
Hanna Batatu's *The Old Social Classes And The Revolutionary Movements Of Iraq*
Christopher Browning's *Ordinary Men: Reserve Police Batallion 101 and the Final Solution in Poland*
Edmund Burke's *Reflections on the Revolution in France*
William Cronon's *Nature's Metropolis: Chicago And The Great West*
Alfred W. Crosby's *The Columbian Exchange*
Hamid Dabashi's *Iran: A People Interrupted*
David Brion Davis's *The Problem of Slavery in the Age of Revolution*
Nathalie Zemon Davis's *The Return of Martin Guerre*
Jared Diamond's *Guns, Germs & Steel: the Fate of Human Societies*
Frank Dikotter's *Mao's Great Famine*
John W Dower's *War Without Mercy: Race And Power In The Pacific War*
W. E. B. Du Bois's *The Souls of Black Folk*
Richard J. Evans's *In Defence of History*
Lucien Febvre's *The Problem of Unbelief in the 16th Century*
Sheila Fitzpatrick's *Everyday Stalinism*

The Macat Library By Discipline

Eric Foner's *Reconstruction: America's Unfinished Revolution, 1863-1877*
Michel Foucault's *Discipline and Punish*
Michel Foucault's *History of Sexuality*
Francis Fukuyama's *The End of History and the Last Man*
John Lewis Gaddis's *We Now Know: Rethinking Cold War History*
Ernest Gellner's *Nations and Nationalism*
Eugene Genovese's *Roll, Jordan, Roll: The World the Slaves Made*
Carlo Ginzburg's *The Night Battles*
Daniel Goldhagen's *Hitler's Willing Executioners*
Jack Goldstone's *Revolution and Rebellion in the Early Modern World*
Antonio Gramsci's *The Prison Notebooks*
Alexander Hamilton, John Jay & James Madison's *The Federalist Papers*
Christopher Hill's *The World Turned Upside Down*
Carole Hillenbrand's *The Crusades: Islamic Perspectives*
Thomas Hobbes's *Leviathan*
Eric Hobsbawm's *The Age Of Revolution*
John A. Hobson's *Imperialism: A Study*
Albert Hourani's *History of the Arab Peoples*
Samuel P. Huntington's *The Clash of Civilizations and the Remaking of World Order*
C. L. R. James's *The Black Jacobins*
Tony Judt's *Postwar: A History of Europe Since 1945*
Ernst Kantorowicz's *The King's Two Bodies: A Study in Medieval Political Theology*
Paul Kennedy's *The Rise and Fall of the Great Powers*
Ian Kershaw's *The "Hitler Myth": Image and Reality in the Third Reich*
John Maynard Keynes's *The General Theory of Employment, Interest and Money*
Charles P. Kindleberger's *Manias, Panics and Crashes*
Martin Luther King Jr's *Why We Can't Wait*
Henry Kissinger's *World Order: Reflections on the Character of Nations and the Course of History*
Thomas Kuhn's *The Structure of Scientific Revolutions*
Georges Lefebvre's *The Coming of the French Revolution*
John Locke's *Two Treatises of Government*
Niccolò Machiavelli's *The Prince*
Thomas Robert Malthus's *An Essay on the Principle of Population*
Mahmood Mamdani's *Citizen and Subject: Contemporary Africa And The Legacy Of Late Colonialism*
Karl Marx's *Capital*
Stanley Milgram's *Obedience to Authority*
John Stuart Mill's *On Liberty*
Thomas Paine's *Common Sense*
Thomas Paine's *Rights of Man*
Geoffrey Parker's *Global Crisis: War, Climate Change and Catastrophe in the Seventeenth Century*
Jonathan Riley-Smith's *The First Crusade and the Idea of Crusading*
Jean-Jacques Rousseau's *The Social Contract*
Joan Wallach Scott's *Gender and the Politics of History*
Theda Skocpol's *States and Social Revolutions*
Adam Smith's *The Wealth of Nations*
Timothy Snyder's *Bloodlands: Europe Between Hitler and Stalin*
Sun Tzu's *The Art of War*
Keith Thomas's *Religion and the Decline of Magic*
Thucydides's *The History of the Peloponnesian War*
Frederick Jackson Turner's *The Significance of the Frontier in American History*
Odd Arne Westad's *The Global Cold War: Third World Interventions And The Making Of Our Times*

LITERATURE

Chinua Achebe's *An Image of Africa: Racism in Conrad's Heart of Darkness*
Roland Barthes's *Mythologies*
Homi K. Bhabha's *The Location of Culture*
Judith Butler's *Gender Trouble*
Simone De Beauvoir's *The Second Sex*
Ferdinand De Saussure's *Course in General Linguistics*
T. S. Eliot's *The Sacred Wood: Essays on Poetry and Criticism*
Zora Neale Huston's *Characteristics of Negro Expression*
Toni Morrison's *Playing in the Dark: Whiteness in the American Literary Imagination*
Edward Said's *Orientalism*
Gayatri Chakravorty Spivak's *Can the Subaltern Speak?*
Mary Wollstonecraft's *A Vindication of the Rights of Women*
Virginia Woolf's *A Room of One's Own*

PHILOSOPHY

Elizabeth Anscombe's *Modern Moral Philosophy*
Hannah Arendt's *The Human Condition*
Aristotle's *Metaphysics*
Aristotle's *Nicomachean Ethics*
Edmund Gettier's *Is Justified True Belief Knowledge?*
Georg Wilhelm Friedrich Hegel's *Phenomenology of Spirit*
David Hume's *Dialogues Concerning Natural Religion*
David Hume's *The Enquiry for Human Understanding*
Immanuel Kant's *Religion within the Boundaries of Mere Reason*
Immanuel Kant's *Critique of Pure Reason*
Søren Kierkegaard's *The Sickness Unto Death*
Søren Kierkegaard's *Fear and Trembling*
C. S. Lewis's *The Abolition of Man*
Alasdair MacIntyre's *After Virtue*
Marcus Aurelius's *Meditations*
Friedrich Nietzsche's *On the Genealogy of Morality*
Friedrich Nietzsche's *Beyond Good and Evil*
Plato's *Republic*
Plato's *Symposium*
Jean-Jacques Rousseau's *The Social Contract*
Gilbert Ryle's *The Concept of Mind*
Baruch Spinoza's *Ethics*
Sun Tzu's *The Art of War*
Ludwig Wittgenstein's *Philosophical Investigations*

POLITICS

Benedict Anderson's *Imagined Communities*
Aristotle's *Politics*
Bernard Bailyn's *The Ideological Origins of the American Revolution*
Edmund Burke's *Reflections on the Revolution in France*
John C. Calhoun's *A Disquisition on Government*
Ha-Joon Chang's *Kicking Away the Ladder*
Hamid Dabashi's *Iran: A People Interrupted*
Hamid Dabashi's *Theology of Discontent: The Ideological Foundation of the Islamic Revolution in Iran*
Robert Dahl's *Democracy and its Critics*
Robert Dahl's *Who Governs?*
David Brion Davis's *The Problem of Slavery in the Age of Revolution*

The Macat Library By Discipline

Alexis De Tocqueville's *Democracy in America*
James Ferguson's *The Anti-Politics Machine*
Frank Dikotter's *Mao's Great Famine*
Sheila Fitzpatrick's *Everyday Stalinism*
Eric Foner's *Reconstruction: America's Unfinished Revolution, 1863-1877*
Milton Friedman's *Capitalism and Freedom*
Francis Fukuyama's *The End of History and the Last Man*
John Lewis Gaddis's *We Now Know: Rethinking Cold War History*
Ernest Gellner's *Nations and Nationalism*
David Graeber's *Debt: the First 5000 Years*
Antonio Gramsci's *The Prison Notebooks*
Alexander Hamilton, John Jay & James Madison's *The Federalist Papers*
Friedrich Hayek's *The Road to Serfdom*
Christopher Hill's *The World Turned Upside Down*
Thomas Hobbes's *Leviathan*
John A. Hobson's *Imperialism: A Study*
Samuel P. Huntington's *The Clash of Civilizations and the Remaking of World Order*
Tony Judt's *Postwar: A History of Europe Since 1945*
David C. Kang's *China Rising: Peace, Power and Order in East Asia*
Paul Kennedy's *The Rise and Fall of Great Powers*
Robert Keohane's *After Hegemony*
Martin Luther King Jr.'s *Why We Can't Wait*
Henry Kissinger's *World Order: Reflections on the Character of Nations and the Course of History*
John Locke's *Two Treatises of Government*
Niccolò Machiavelli's *The Prince*
Thomas Robert Malthus's *An Essay on the Principle of Population*
Mahmood Mamdani's *Citizen and Subject: Contemporary Africa And The Legacy Of Late Colonialism*
Karl Marx's *Capital*
John Stuart Mill's *On Liberty*
John Stuart Mill's *Utilitarianism*
Hans Morgenthau's *Politics Among Nations*
Thomas Paine's *Common Sense*
Thomas Paine's *Rights of Man*
Thomas Piketty's *Capital in the Twenty-First Century*
Robert D. Putman's *Bowling Alone*
John Rawls's *Theory of Justice*
Jean-Jacques Rousseau's *The Social Contract*
Theda Skocpol's *States and Social Revolutions*
Adam Smith's *The Wealth of Nations*
Sun Tzu's *The Art of War*
Henry David Thoreau's *Civil Disobedience*
Thucydides's *The History of the Peloponnesian War*
Kenneth Waltz's *Theory of International Politics*
Max Weber's *Politics as a Vocation*
Odd Arne Westad's *The Global Cold War: Third World Interventions And The Making Of Our Times*

POSTCOLONIAL STUDIES

Roland Barthes's *Mythologies*
Frantz Fanon's *Black Skin, White Masks*
Homi K. Bhabha's *The Location of Culture*
Gustavo Gutiérrez's *A Theology of Liberation*
Edward Said's *Orientalism*
Gayatri Chakravorty Spivak's *Can the Subaltern Speak?*

PSYCHOLOGY

Gordon Allport's *The Nature of Prejudice*
Alan Baddeley & Graham Hitch's *Aggression: A Social Learning Analysis*
Albert Bandura's *Aggression: A Social Learning Analysis*
Leon Festinger's *A Theory of Cognitive Dissonance*
Sigmund Freud's *The Interpretation of Dreams*
Betty Friedan's *The Feminine Mystique*
Michael R. Gottfredson & Travis Hirschi's *A General Theory of Crime*
Eric Hoffer's *The True Believer: Thoughts on the Nature of Mass Movements*
William James's *Principles of Psychology*
Elizabeth Loftus's *Eyewitness Testimony*
A. H. Maslow's *A Theory of Human Motivation*
Stanley Milgram's *Obedience to Authority*
Steven Pinker's *The Better Angels of Our Nature*
Oliver Sacks's *The Man Who Mistook His Wife For a Hat*
Richard Thaler & Cass Sunstein's *Nudge: Improving Decisions About Health, Wealth and Happiness*
Amos Tversky's *Judgment under Uncertainty: Heuristics and Biases*
Philip Zimbardo's *The Lucifer Effect*

SCIENCE

Rachel Carson's *Silent Spring*
William Cronon's *Nature's Metropolis: Chicago And The Great West*
Alfred W. Crosby's *The Columbian Exchange*
Charles Darwin's *On the Origin of Species*
Richard Dawkin's *The Selfish Gene*
Thomas Kuhn's *The Structure of Scientific Revolutions*
Geoffrey Parker's *Global Crisis: War, Climate Change and Catastrophe in the Seventeenth Century*
Mathis Wackernagel & William Rees's *Our Ecological Footprint*

SOCIOLOGY

Michelle Alexander's *The New Jim Crow: Mass Incarceration in the Age of Colorblindness*
Gordon Allport's *The Nature of Prejudice*
Albert Bandura's *Aggression: A Social Learning Analysis*
Hanna Batatu's *The Old Social Classes And The Revolutionary Movements Of Iraq*
Ha-Joon Chang's *Kicking Away the Ladder*
W. E. B. Du Bois's *The Souls of Black Folk*
Émile Durkheim's *On Suicide*
Frantz Fanon's *Black Skin, White Masks*
Frantz Fanon's *The Wretched of the Earth*
Eric Foner's *Reconstruction: America's Unfinished Revolution, 1863-1877*
Eugene Genovese's *Roll, Jordan, Roll: The World the Slaves Made*
Jack Goldstone's *Revolution and Rebellion in the Early Modern World*
Antonio Gramsci's *The Prison Notebooks*
Richard Herrnstein & Charles A Murray's *The Bell Curve: Intelligence and Class Structure in American Life*
Eric Hoffer's *The True Believer: Thoughts on the Nature of Mass Movements*
Jane Jacobs's *The Death and Life of Great American Cities*
Robert Lucas's *Why Doesn't Capital Flow from Rich to Poor Countries?*
Jay Macleod's *Ain't No Makin' It: Aspirations and Attainment in a Low Income Neighborhood*
Elaine May's *Homeward Bound: American Families in the Cold War Era*
Douglas McGregor's *The Human Side of Enterprise*
C. Wright Mills's *The Sociological Imagination*

The Macat Library By Discipline

Thomas Piketty's *Capital in the Twenty-First Century*
Robert D. Putman's *Bowling Alone*
David Riesman's *The Lonely Crowd: A Study of the Changing American Character*
Edward Said's *Orientalism*
Joan Wallach Scott's *Gender and the Politics of History*
Theda Skocpol's *States and Social Revolutions*
Max Weber's *The Protestant Ethic and the Spirit of Capitalism*

THEOLOGY

Augustine's *Confessions*
Benedict's *Rule of St Benedict*
Gustavo Gutiérrez's *A Theology of Liberation*
Carole Hillenbrand's *The Crusades: Islamic Perspectives*
David Hume's *Dialogues Concerning Natural Religion*
Immanuel Kant's *Religion within the Boundaries of Mere Reason*
Ernst Kantorowicz's *The King's Two Bodies: A Study in Medieval Political Theology*
Søren Kierkegaard's *The Sickness Unto Death*
C. S. Lewis's *The Abolition of Man*
Saba Mahmood's *The Politics of Piety: The Islamic Revival and the Feminist Subject*
Baruch Spinoza's *Ethics*
Keith Thomas's *Religion and the Decline of Magic*

COMING SOON

Chris Argyris's *The Individual and the Organisation*
Seyla Benhabib's *The Rights of Others*
Walter Benjamin's *The Work Of Art in the Age of Mechanical Reproduction*
John Berger's *Ways of Seeing*
Pierre Bourdieu's *Outline of a Theory of Practice*
Mary Douglas's *Purity and Danger*
Roland Dworkin's *Taking Rights Seriously*
James G. March's *Exploration and Exploitation in Organisational Learning*
Ikujiro Nonaka's *A Dynamic Theory of Organizational Knowledge Creation*
Griselda Pollock's *Vision and Difference*
Amartya Sen's *Inequality Re-Examined*
Susan Sontag's *On Photography*
Yasser Tabbaa's *The Transformation of Islamic Art*
Ludwig von Mises's *Theory of Money and Credit*

Macat Disciplines

Access the greatest ideas and thinkers across entire disciplines, including

Postcolonial Studies

Roland Barthes's *Mythologies*
Frantz Fanon's *Black Skin, White Masks*
Homi K. Bhabha's *The Location of Culture*
Gustavo Gutiérrez's *A Theology of Liberation*
Edward Said's *Orientalism*
Gayatri Chakravorty Spivak's *Can the Subaltern Speak?*

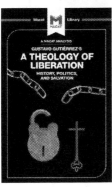

Macat analyses are available from all good bookshops and libraries.

Access hundreds of analyses through one, multimedia tool.
Join free for one month **library.macat.com**

Macat Disciplines

Access the greatest ideas and thinkers across entire disciplines, including

AFRICANA STUDIES

Chinua Achebe's *An Image of Africa: Racism in Conrad's Heart of Darkness*

W. E. B. Du Bois's *The Souls of Black Folk*

Zora Neale Hurston's *Characteristics of Negro Expression*

Martin Luther King Jr.'s *Why We Can't Wait*

Toni Morrison's *Playing in the Dark: Whiteness in the American Literary Imagination*

Macat analyses are available from all good bookshops and libraries.

Access hundreds of analyses through one, multimedia tool.
Join free for one month **library.macat.com**

Macat Pairs

Analyse historical and modern issues from opposite sides of an argument. Pairs include:

ARE WE FUNDAMENTALLY GOOD - OR BAD?

Steven Pinker's
The Better Angels of Our Nature

Stephen Pinker's gloriously optimistic 2011 book argues that, despite humanity's biological tendency toward violence, we are, in fact, less violent today than ever before. To prove his case, Pinker lays out pages of detailed statistical evidence. For him, much of the credit for the decline goes to the eighteenth-century Enlightenment movement, whose ideas of liberty, tolerance, and respect for the value of human life filtered down through society and affected how people thought. That psychological change led to behavioral change—and overall we became more peaceful. Critics countered that humanity could never overcome the biological urge toward violence; others argued that Pinker's statistics were flawed.

Philip Zimbardo's
The Lucifer Effect

Some psychologists believe those who commit cruelty are innately evil. Zimbardo disagrees. In *The Lucifer Effect*, he argues that sometimes good people do evil things simply because of the situations they find themselves in, citing many historical examples to illustrate his point. Zimbardo details his 1971 Stanford prison experiment, where ordinary volunteers playing guards in a mock prison rapidly became abusive. But he also describes the tortures committed by US army personnel in Iraq's Abu Ghraib prison in 2003—and how he himself testified in defence of one of those guards. committed by US army personnel in Iraq's Abu Ghraib prison in 2003—and how he himself testified in defence of one of those guards.

Macat analyses are available from all good bookshops and libraries.

Access hundreds of analyses through one, multimedia tool.
Join free for one month **library.macat.com**

Macat Pairs

Analyse historical and modern issues from opposite sides of an argument. Pairs include:

RACE AND IDENTITY

Zora Neale Hurston's
Characteristics of Negro Expression

Using material collected on anthropological expeditions to the South, Zora Neale Hurston explains how expression in African American culture in the early twentieth century departs from the art of white America. At the time, African American art was often criticized for copying white culture. For Hurston, this criticism misunderstood how art works. European tradition views art as something fixed. But Hurston describes a creative process that is alive, ever-changing, and largely improvisational. She maintains that African American art works through a process called 'mimicry'—where an imitated object or verbal pattern, for example, is reshaped and altered until it becomes something new, novel—and worthy of attention.

Frantz Fanon's
Black Skin, White Masks

Black Skin, White Masks offers a radical analysis of the psychological effects of colonization on the colonized.

Fanon witnessed the effects of colonization first hand both in his birthplace, Martinique, and again later in life when he worked as a psychiatrist in another French colony, Algeria. His text is uncompromising in form and argument. He dissects the dehumanizing effects of colonialism, arguing that it destroys the native sense of identity, forcing people to adapt to an alien set of values—including a core belief that they are inferior. This results in deep psychological trauma.

Fanon's work played a pivotal role in the civil rights movements of the 1960s.

Macat Disciplines

Access the greatest ideas and thinkers across entire disciplines, including

INEQUALITY

Ha-Joon Chang's, *Kicking Away the Ladder*

David Graeber's, *Debt: The First 5000 Years*

Robert E. Lucas's, *Why Doesn't Capital Flow from Rich To Poor Countries?*

Thomas Piketty's, *Capital in the Twenty-First Century*

Amartya Sen's, *Inequality Re-Examined*

Mahbub Ul Haq's, *Reflections on Human Development*

Macat analyses are available from all good bookshops and libraries.

Access hundreds of analyses through one, multimedia tool.
Join free for one month **library.macat.com**

Macat Disciplines

Access the greatest ideas and thinkers across entire disciplines, including

CRIMINOLOGY

Michelle Alexander's
The New Jim Crow: Mass Incarceration in the Age of Colorblindness

Michael R. Gottfredson & Travis Hirschi's
A General Theory of Crime

Elizabeth Loftus's
Eyewitness Testimony

Richard Herrnstein & Charles A. Murray's
The Bell Curve: Intelligence and Class Structure in American Life

Jay Macleod's
Ain't No Makin' It: Aspirations and Attainment in a Low-Income Neighborhood

Philip Zimbardo's
The Lucifer Effect

Macat Disciplines

Access the greatest ideas and thinkers across entire disciplines, including

GLOBALIZATION

Arjun Appadurai's, *Modernity at Large: Cultural Dimensions of Globalisation*

James Ferguson's, *The Anti-Politics Machine*

Geert Hofstede's, *Culture's Consequences*

Amartya Sen's, *Development as Freedom*

Macat Disciplines

Access the greatest ideas and thinkers across entire disciplines, including

MAN AND THE ENVIRONMENT

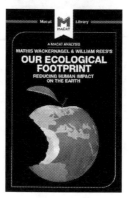

The Brundtland Report's, *Our Common Future*
Rachel Carson's, *Silent Spring*
James Lovelock's, *Gaia: A New Look at Life on Earth*
Mathis Wackernagel & William Rees's, *Our Ecological Footprint*

Macat analyses are available from all good bookshops and libraries.

Access hundreds of analyses through one, multimedia tool.
Join free for one month **library.macat.com**

Macat Disciplines

Access the greatest ideas and thinkers
across entire disciplines, including

THE FUTURE OF DEMOCRACY

Robert A. Dahl's, *Democracy and Its Critics*
Robert A. Dahl's, *Who Governs?*
Alexis De Toqueville's, *Democracy in America*
Niccolò Machiavelli's, *The Prince*
John Stuart Mill's, *On Liberty*
Robert D. Putnam's, *Bowling Alone*
Jean-Jacques Rousseau's, *The Social Contract*
Henry David Thoreau's, *Civil Disobedience*

Macat analyses are available from all good bookshops and libraries.

Access hundreds of analyses through one, multimedia tool.
Join free for one month **library.macat.com**

Macat Disciplines

Access the greatest ideas and thinkers across entire disciplines, including

TOTALITARIANISM

Sheila Fitzpatrick's, *Everyday Stalinism*
Ian Kershaw's, *The "Hitler Myth"*
Timothy Snyder's, *Bloodlands*

Macat Pairs

Analyse historical and modern issues from opposite sides of an argument. Pairs include:

INTERNATIONAL RELATIONS IN THE 21ˢᵀ CENTURY

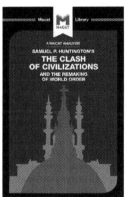

Samuel P. Huntington's
The Clash of Civilisations

In his highly influential 1996 book, Huntington offers a vision of a post-Cold War world in which conflict takes place not between competing ideologies but between cultures. The worst clash, he argues, will be between the Islamic world and the West: the West's arrogance and belief that its culture is a "gift" to the world will come into conflict with Islam's obstinacy and concern that its culture is under attack from a morally decadent "other."

Clash inspired much debate between different political schools of thought. But its greatest impact came in helping define American foreign policy in the wake of the 2001 terrorist attacks in New York and Washington.

Francis Fukuyama's
The End of History and the Last Man

Published in 1992, *The End of History and the Last Man* argues that capitalist democracy is the final destination for all societies. Fukuyama believed democracy triumphed during the Cold War because it lacks the "fundamental contradictions" inherent in communism and satisfies our yearning for freedom and equality. Democracy therefore marks the endpoint in the evolution of ideology, and so the "end of history." There will still be "events," but no fundamental change in ideology.

Printed in the United States
by Baker & Taylor Publisher Services